CRITICAL ACCLAIM FOR THE WORKS OF JAMES RADA, JR.

Saving Shallmar

"But Saving Shallmar's Christmas story is a tale of compassion and charity, and the will to help fellow human beings not only survive, but also be ready to spring into action when a new opportunity presents itself. Bittersweet yet heartwarming, Saving Shallmar is a wonderful Christmas season story for readers of all ages and backgrounds, highly recommended."

- *Small Press Bookwatch*

Battlefield Angels

"Rada describes women religious who selflessly performed life-saving work in often miserable conditions and thereby gained the admiration and respect of countless contemporaries. In so doing, Rada offers an appealing narrative and an entry point into the wealth of sources kept by the sisters."

- *Catholic News Service*

Canawlers

"A powerful, thoughtful and fascinating historical novel, Canawlers documents author James Rada, Jr. as a writer of considerable and deftly expressed storytelling talent."

- *Midwest Book Review*

D0932699

Between Rail and River

"The book is an enjoyable, clean family read, with characters young and old for a broad-based appeal to both teens and adults. Between Rail and River also provides a unique, regional appeal, as it teaches about a particular group of people, ordinary working 'canawlers' in a story that goes beyond the usual coverage of life during the Civil War."

- *Historical Fiction Review*

Canawlers

"James Rada, of Cumberland, has written a historical novel for high-schoolers and adults, which relates the adventures, hardships and ultimate tragedy of a family of boaters on the C&O Canal. … The tale moves quickly and should hold the attention of readers looking for an imaginative adventure set on the canal at a critical time in history."

- *Along the Towpath*

OTHER BOOKS BY JAMES RADA, JR.

Fiction

Between Rail and River

Canawlers

October Mourning

The Rain Man

Non-Fiction

Echoes of War Drums: The Civil War in Mountain Maryland

Battlefield Angels: The Daughters of Charity Work
as Civil War Nurses

Looking Back: True Stories of Mountain Maryland

Looking Back II: More True Stories of Mountain Maryland

No North, No South…: The Grand Reunion at the 50th Anniversary of the Battle of Gettysburg

Saving Shallmar: Christmas Spirit in a Coal Town

For Sam, my dreamer

BEYOND THE BATTLEFIELD
Stories from Gettysburg's Rich History

by
James Rada, Jr.

LEGACY
PUBLISHING

A division of AIM Publishing Group

BEYOND THE BATTLEFIELD:
STORIES FROM GETTYSBURG'S RICH HISTORY

Published by Legacy Publishing, a division of AIM Publishing
Group.
Gettysburg, Pennsylvania.
Copyright © 2014 by James Rada, Jr.
All rights reserved.
Printed in the United States of America.
First printing: March 2014.

Portions of this book first appeared in the *Gettysburg Times,
Celebrate Gettysburg, The Gettysburg Experience, Pennsylvania Magazine* and *Pennsylvania Heritage.* This edition replaces
and incorporates a smaller e-book edition published previously.

ISBN: 978-0-61598025-6

Main cover photo courtesy of the Library of Congress.

LEGACY
PUBLISHING

315 Oak Lane • Gettysburg, Pennsylvania 17325

CONTENTS

AUTHOR'S INTRODUCTION

Gettysburg, Pa., is nearly synonymous with the Civil War. That's not surprising since the largest battle of the war was fought here during the first three days in July 1863. It was also the turning point of the Civil War.

While the battle certainly deserves the attention that it receives, Gettysburg has been around for much longer than those three days and has had a lot of interesting things happen, which I have discovered living here. A U.S. President called Gettysburg home and so did a Hall of Fame baseball pitcher. There are stories of Indians, ghosts and tanks.

I have collected some of those stories here in Beyond the Battlefield: True Stories from Gettysburg's Rich History. They have appeared in magazines like the *Gettysburg Times, The Gettysburg Experience* and *Celebrate Gettysburg*.

They should also give you a good feel for the scope of Gettysburg's history. I hope you enjoy them.

James Rada, Jr.
Gettysburg, Pa.

1

WASHINGTON SLEPT HERE

Though George Washington never visited Adams County, he traveled through towns that would eventually become part of the county named for his vice president.

Washington traveled through the county twice; once during his first term in office and once during his second term.

The new U.S. government passed a tax on distilled spirits in 1790 in order to raise revenue. This didn't sit well with farmers who distilled liquor from corn and grain leftover from the harvest. The farmers could then sell it or trade it for an extra source of income and they did not want to have to pay a tax on it.

Western Pennsylvania residents were particularly vehement in their opposition. Beginning in 1791, resolutions were passed in various municipalities saying that any official who attempted to enforce the tax would be ostracized.

"Collectors were tarred, feathered, whipped, blindfolded and tied in the forests. One they stripped, burned with a hot iron in a blacksmith shop and then tarred and feathered. A collector's house was broken into and the family terrified and abused," the *Gettysburg Times* reported in 1904.

The violence peaked in July 1794 when citizens attacked the home of tax inspector General John Neville when the U.S. government attempted to serve writs on distillers who hadn't paid the whiskey tax.

Washington first tried to negotiate with the citizens through peace commissioners. When that failed, he called on the region's governors to send militia to put down the rebellion. Washington rode at the head of the 13,000 troops to put down the rebellion. A confrontation never happened, though, because the rebels simply dispersed, cowed by the militia.

It was on his return from this non-confrontation that Washington passed through Adams County (it was still part of York County at the time) in late October 1794. "The route according to the best authorities was by the pike over the mountains, through Hilltown, Mummasburg, and on through Hunterstown, New Oxford and Abbottstown, until he reached Wrights' Ferry over the Susquehanna," the *Gettysburg Times* reported.

George Washington visited Adams County twice and even spent the night at this tavern, which is now a private home. From the author's collection.

At one point, Washington and his entourage stopped at the stone tavern at the junction of the Arendtsville Road with the old Shippensburg Road (it is now the intersection of Goldenville Road and Russell Tavern Road). The group spent the night there and also ate their meals in the tavern.

"Tradition says the President stopped there and was entertained, and that his presence became noised about and quite a number of the people of the vicinity gathered there and saw the President before he took his departure," the *Gettysburg Times* reported.

By this time, news had filtered out of Western Pennsylvania about the non-rebellion, but people still wanted to hear from someone who had been there about what had "really" happened.

As Washington was preparing to leave, the tavern owner, whose last name was Russell, approached the President and asked what the army was going to do.

The tall President stared at the tavern owner for a moment, then he grinned and leaned down so that he was close to Russell's ear.

"Can you keep a secret?" Washington asked.

Russell assured the President that he could indeed keep a secret. "Then [Washington] turned away, took up his journey and Landlord Russell was no wiser of the secret to be kept," the newspaper reported.

The stone house still stands and is a private residence. The Daughters of the American Revolution placed a plaque in front of the house noting its historical significance.

2

THE NIGHT THE SKY FELL IN GETTYSBURG

The old Adams County jail wasn't the most secure of prisons. Early in the morning of November 12, 1833, a convicted murderer was so scared that he broke out of the prison, according to the History of Adams County published in 1886. Though the man was free from prison, he still wore shackles. He ran to the nearest blacksmith shop and filed them off. Then, "as he forgot to come back and give himself up to be hanged, it may be inferred he is still fleeing from the 'stars' that do not pursue," according to the *History of Adams County*.

Few people probably even noticed the killer's escape that evening. Their eyes were turned to the heavens watching the reason the man had become scared enough to make a run for it.

"The whole heavens appeared to be illuminated by countless meteors, of different sizes, which darted frequently horizontally, leaving long trains, but generally fell silently to the ground, resembling, as some term it, large flakes of snow, or as if it were 'snowing stars,'" the *Gettysburg Compiler* reported.

Many people reported beginning to see the falling stars around dusk the day before but the peak of activity seems to have been in the hours before dawn on the 12th. The *Gettysburg Compiler* called it "one of the most splendid and awful spectacles the mind can conceive of, was witnessed in the heavens."

The murderer wasn't the only one fearing the stars that morning. The Carlisle Volunteer noted that the sight of thousands of fiery trails in the sky started people predicting all sorts of dire consequences. "One remarked it was occasioned by the removal of Deposites from the U.S. Bank!—another, that there would be a division of the Union!!—and a third, that it was a sure sign of the rapid approach of cold weather!!!" the newspaper reported.

It wasn't a prediction of the Apocalypse, though. The meteor shower was the Leonid Meteor Shower. It is caused in part by the comet Tempel-Tuttle, which had yet to be discovered in 1833. The comet passes the Earth every 33 years and around mid-November, the Earth moves through the stream of particles and debris that the comet leaves behind.

The 1833 Leonid Meteor Shower frightened the residents of Adams County. Courtesy of Wikimedia Commons.

The 1833 meteor shower was one of the more-spectacular ones seen throughout America east of the Rocky Mountains. Many newspapers reported on the event.

The *Gettysburg Compiler* described it this way: "To form some idea of the phenomenon, the reader may imagine a constant succession of the fire balls, resembling sky rockets, radiating in all directions from a point in the heavens near the zenith, and following the arch of the sky towards the horizon. They proceeded to various distances from the radiating point, leaving after them a vivid streak of light, and usually exploding before they disappeared. The balls were of various sizes and degrees of splendor. The flashes of light, though less intense than lightning, were so bright as to awaken many people in their beds, and many were alarmed, and astonished every person who beheld it."

The variation in intensity comes from slight deviations in the path and size of the dust cloud. The deeper the earth enters it the more spectacular the meteor shower. Other big years for the meteor shower were in 1866 and 1965. No meteors were seen in 1899, which started speculation that the meteor had changed its path. However it returned again in 1932.

3

STUDEBAKER'S GETTYSBURG ROOTS

Say the word "Studebaker" and most people will think of the classic 20th Century automobile manufacturer. The Studebaker Automobile Company began manufacturing electric automobiles in 1902. Thomas Edison gave the cars a publicity boost when he bought the second one the company manufactured, according to the Studebaker National Museum. The company began making gasoline-powered automobiles in 1904.

During its existence, the company introduced a number of well-known cars to the market such as the 1939 Champion, the 1947 Starlight Coupe, the 1950 "Bullet Nose", the 1953 Starliner Hardtop and the 1963 Avanti. The last Studebaker rolled off the line in Hamilton, Ontario, Canada, in March 1966.

However, the Studebaker Company has a history that dates back even further and that is where Gettysburg plays a role.

The Staudenbecker family emigrated from Solingen, Germany in 1736 and arrived in Philadelphia where their name was Americanized to Studebaker. One of the first generation of American-born Studebakers was John S. Studebaker who was born in Getty's Town in 1799. He married Rebecca Mohler in 1820. They eventually had five sons and five daughters. The boys were Henry, Clement, John M., Peter and Jacob. Of these sons, John M. was born in Gettysburg on October 10, 1833.

The Studebakers moved to Ohio in 1836. John M. sought his fortune in California during the Gold Rush and wound up manufacturing wheelbarrows for the miners. Meanwhile, Henry and Clement opened a wagon-building and blacksmith shop in 1852 in South Bend, Ind. John returned from California in 1858 with $8,000 in gold and bought his brother Henry's interest in the Studebaker Wagon Company.

The company grew during the Civil War as the Studebakers built wagons for the federal government. Following the war, the company incorporated in 1868 as the Studebaker Brothers Manufacturing Company with Clement, John and Peter as the owners and Clement as the first president, according to the German-American History and Heritage web site.

The five Studebaker brothers. Standing, from left to right: Peter and Jacob. Seated, left to right: Clem, Henry and John M. Courtesy of Wikimedia Commons.

By December 1901, John M. was 68 years old and the last surviving member of the original founders. "That same year, there was a Motor Show in Chicago, which was not far from South Bend, and John Mohler [Studebaker] attended, knowing full well that it represented the future of the Studebaker company. But while Studebaker realized the automobile was the future, he thought that it was electric cars, not gasoline, that would get him there," according to the Automotive Hall of Fame web site.

John urged his son-in-law, Fred Fish, to move the company into manufacturing electric automobiles, which he did the following year.

As the company grew, it stopped manufacturing electric vehicles and wagons in 1911. John was reluctant to stop one of the company's founding product lines, though.

He said, "The automobile has come to stay. But when a man has no business, it is a rather expensive luxury, and I would advise no man, be he farmer or merchant, to buy one until he has sufficient income to keep it up. A horse and buggy will afford a great deal of enjoyment ....," according to the Automotive Hall of Fame.

John was still serving as the honorary president of the company when he died in 1917 at the age of 83. The headline on the *South Bend Saturday Tribune* proclaimed: "DEATH CLAIMS LAST OF FIVE BIG BROTHERS J.M. STUDEBAKER PASSES AWAY IN MIDST OF FAMILY. END WAS VERY PEACEFUL. MANUFAC-TURER AND PHILANTHROPIST, CONSCIOUS TO THE LAST, DISCUSSES BUSINESS ALMOST UP TO FINAL HOUR."

John was inducted into the Automotive Hall of Fame in 2005. Studebaker automobiles still continue, too. A new Studebaker Motor Company opened in 2002.

4

UP, UP AND AWAY IN MY BEAUTIFUL BALLOON!

The October winds gusted through Gettysburg in 1842, sending loose hats flying into the air. John Wise considered it good news. It would help him take flight for the thirty-ninth time in his hot air balloon.

He stoked the fire that generated the heat that was slowly inflating the enormous balloon. Then he moved on to stowing his ballast and grappling hook in the basket.

At last the moment came to launch himself into the heavens. As he prepared to step into the basket that hung below the balloon, John McClellan, a young man in his early thirties stepped forward.

McClellan wanted to know whether two men could go up at once in the balloon.

"On receiving a negative reply, Mr. McClellan seeming much disappointed-said he was determined to have a ride: and inquired the price at which Mr. Wise would permit him to make the voyage alone," reported *The York Gazette* in October 1842.

"One hundred dollars," Wise told him, thinking that such an expensive price would discourage McClellan's enthusiasm.

"I will give you fifty dollars!" McClellan countered.

It was still a good sum so Wise said, "Agreed—fork over!"

McClellan did so and then climbed into the basket. Wise gave him some rudimentary instruction on how a balloon operated. McClellan soaked it all in and then gave the order to "cut loose!"

Wise thought that the joke had gone far enough and told McClellan it was time to get out. "But he refused to do so, and insisted that he had regularly hired and paid for a passage 'in this boat,' and go he would," *The York Gazette* reported.

Wise relented, particularly since he didn't want to relent his fifty dollars. He also apparently believed that the gusting winds would cause McClellan airsickness. Wise let the balloon begin a short climb, still connected to the earth by a rope.

"But this was no go; and thinking he has as good a start as he would ever have, Mr. McClellan cut the rope and was off!" reported *The York Gazette.*

According to the newspaper, McClellan quickly reached a height of two miles. This is doubtful because two miles is close to the height where a hot air balloon operator would have needed oxygen and a very warm coat. Most comfortable balloon rides take place around 2,000 feet.

Sitting in the basket, McClellan had a sense of sitting still while the world moved beneath him as can be seen in his description of the journey. "...Gettysburg passed off towards Hagerstown, Abbotts-town, Oxford, and Berlin, strolling about; and soon after, just ahead of him, he saw old York coming full tilt up the turnpike toward him, apparently taking an afternoon's walk to Gettysburg," reported *The York Gazette.*

Now, McClellan began to get worried. He was moving along so quickly that he wasn't sure where he would wind up.

"Having determined to stop at York, and fearing, from the re-markable speed at which our usually staid and sober town was travel-ling, that she would pass under his balloon, and give him the slip, he pulled the string attached to the safety valve, in order to let off a por-tion of the gas," the newspaper reported.

However, he pulled too hard on the valve and it tore loose com-pletely. The hot gas inside the balloon began escaping and the balloon plummeted toward the earth.

"The escape of the gas was distinctly seen from York; and as the balloon neared the earth it had lost its rotundity and appeared to the gazers here to come down heavily like a wet sheet," the newspaper reported.

The deflating balloon began acting like a parachute, slowing the descent. McClellan gathered his senses and was beginning to consider throwing out the rest of the ballast and the grappling iron when the basket hit the ground five miles outside of York.

McClellan was shaken but unharmed. Though he would live an-other 47 years and become a successful Gettysburg businessman, Bri-an A. Kennell wrote in *Beyond the Gatehouse: Gettysburg's Ever-*

green Cemetery that "…the eccentric McClellan is best remembered for his infamous balloon ride from Gettysburg to York in 1842."

John McClellan, a young man in his early thirties, rode a hot air balloon, such as the one pictured above, from Gettysburg to York in 1842.

The story was even published in other newspapers in 1842 including the October 12, 1842 edition of *The Massachusetts Spy.* Scott Smelser, who sells original antique newspapers at 17 on the Square showed me copy of *The Massachusetts Spy* that contained this story.

5

THE ODD FELLOWS OF GETTYSBURG

Gettysburg has had its share of heroes, famous people and Odd Fellows. Yes, that's Odd Fellows with a capital O and F.

Gettysburg's first Odd Fellow came from Chambersburg.

"At the time of its institution, carriage building was one of the principal industries of Gettysburg. Robert Davidson Armor, a member of Columbus, No. 75, of Chambersburg, came to Gettysburg to work at his trade of silver plating in carriage making. He, as [James] Wildey, missed the meeting of his lodge," the *Gettysburg Times* reported during the centennial celebration of the Getty Lodge of the Independent Order of Odd Fellows.

The Odd Fellows is fraternal order that dates back to the 1600's in Europe. As with the founding date, there is some dispute over where the name came from. According to the Odd Fellows web site, the first Odd Fellows were tradesmen who didn't belong to the traditional trade guilds of the time and banded together to form their own union.

"At the time of industrialization in England, 'Fellow' from numerous 'Odd' trades gathered together and formed a fraternity to protect and care for their members and communities at a time when there was no welfare state, trade unions and National Health Insurance. They would work together to help each other in times of sickness and distress, whether it was rebuilding a barn that had burned, or putting in a new crop after a devastating season. Such helpers came to be known as 'Odd fellows,' so named by general population who also thought they were 'an odd bunch of fellows' who would behave in such a selfless and seemingly impractical fashion."

However, the first meeting of the Independent Order of Odd Fellows in Gettysburg was on September 16, 1845. Worldwide, there were about 30,000 members. Membership grew quickly to one million members by 1900.

The Getty Lodge operated continuously except for two weeks around the Battle of Gettysburg in 1863. Over the years, the organization met in places like McConaughy's Hall, Buehler Hall, Winter Building and the First National Bank.

Members of the Getty Lodge of the Independent Order of Odd Fellows in the early 20th Century. Courtesy of the Adams County Historical Society.

During the Civil War, 130 Gettysburg Odd Fellows fought in the war as surgeons, musicians and soldiers. They also served anywhere from a lowly private to colonel.

By the time the Getty Lodge turned 100, Adams County had five Odd Fellow lodges: the Getty Lodge, the York Springs Lodge, the Sylvania Lodge in Littlestown, the Montana Lodge in Bendersville and the Valley Home Lodge in Fairfield.

"In its early stages the order conferred five degrees upon its novitiates, but of recent years this has been reduced to three—namely the degrees of Friendship, Love and Truth, which are exemplified with beautiful dramatic work," the *Gettysburg Times* reported.

The Odd Fellows would send checks to the widows of its members. Supporting arthritis research was one of the causes that Odd Fellows supported nationwide. The Getty Lodge also contributed to the Lutheran Home in Gettysburg and funded trips for students to visit the battlefield.

However, by the latter Twentieth Century, membership in fraternal organizations had fallen off considerably. There were only 360,000 Odd Fellows by 1996 and the Getty Lodge had only 16 members.

One of the Lodge's last members was 84-year-old Philip Neth, who had been a member of the Getty Lodge since the 1930's. He said during an interview with the *Hanover Sun* that one of reasons for the shrinking membership was, "Today people are used to all that being done by government agencies. A hundred and 150 years ago, it was relations, societies like ours, churches, and neighbors that took care of people."

While the Independent Order of Odd Fellows is still around today, the closest lodge to Gettysburg is in York Springs.

6

ADAMS COUNTY'S FIRST PRISON BURNS DOWN

On the evening of January 7, 1850, a young man in Gettysburg walked home after he "had been out late interviewing his sweetheart," according to the *History of Adams County* published in 1886. As he walked along High Street around 3 a.m., he saw fire coming out of the second-floor front windows of the county jail.

"The alarm was at once given, and our citizens speedily collected. But all efforts to subdue the flames were fruitless," the *Gettysburg Compiler* reported.

This is not to say that the citizens didn't try. They had no choice. Two men were incarcerated in the jail at the time. Isaac Musselman and John Toner were both considered insane and confined in cells in the jail.

Townsmen with no special firefighting equipment and aid by only blankets and buckets of water rushed to Musselman's cell first because that was determined to be where the fire had started.

"When his apartment was reached, it was found to be all on fire, and that an entrance would be attended with certain death," the *Compiler* reported.

They then opened the door to Toner's cell. Though not on fire, the cell was so filled with smoke that they couldn't breathe or see inside. From outside the jail, someone broke the cell's window to ventilate the room. This allowed the men to enter and retrieve Toner, but he was dead from smoke inhalation.

The fire continued to burn. "Everything that would burn about the building, the fire consumed, nothing is now left of it, but the bare blackened walls," the *Compiler* reported.

The Adams County Jail built to replace the jail that burned down in 1850. The building now houses the Gettysburg Borough offices. Courtesy of the Adams County Historical Society.

While the building hadn't been a high-security prison, it had served its purpose. "The jail, after a fashion, held the few criminals committed to its keeping; that is, like all jails, held some, while others escaped," according to the *History of Adams County*.

Sheriff William Fickes, who had been sheriff since 1848, lost around $500, a considerable amount of money at the time.

Once the fire burned itself out, the men were able to retrieve Musselman's "mutilated and blackened" body. It was buried in the St. James Lutheran Church graveyard.

Firefighting at the time consisted of all able-bodied men in an area answering fire calls, grabbing a bucket and rushing to the site of the fire to help on the bucket brigade lines or to help on the fire pumps. In some jurisdictions, it was a town law that men do so. While apparently plenty of people showed up at the fire scene, not all of them were willing to help.

"We deem this a proper occasion to remind people who go to fires just to see, that their 'room is better than their presence.' Their idleness, when the exertion of every one is required, is catching, and does harm," the *Compiler* reported.

The jail was rebuilt the following year, though Fickes would not be serving as sheriff at that point. John Scott was elected the new sheriff and began serving in 1851. The new county jail served the county until it became the county library in 1949 and is currently the location of the Gettysburg Borough offices.

7

THE DAUGHTERS OF CHARITY NURSING AT GETTYSBURG

The Union soldiers who had camped on the property around St. Joseph's Academy in Emmitsburg, Md., for a few days before the Battle of Gettysburg had been tired, yes, but they had been whole. The men who trudged through Emmitsburg returning from the battle were beaten down and torn apart by three days of fighting.

Gen. Robert E. Lee began his withdrawal toward Williamsport, Md., on July 3, 1863. His train of wounded soldiers, wagons and artillery stretched more than fourteen miles.[1] A few of the stragglers took brief refuge with the Daughters of Charity of Emmitsburg at St. Joseph's Academy before continuing South. Sister Camilla O'Keefe wrote, "On Sunday morning some poor straggling Confederates came down our way. ... They got a good warm breakfast here, after which they set out for part unknown to any but themselves."[2]

The Catholic sisters would do much more than simply feed retreating soldiers, though. As Father William Barnaby Faherty pointed out, "The country had only 600 trained nurses at the start of the Civil War. All were Catholic nuns. This is one of the best-kept secrets in our nation's history."[3]

The best-kept secret

As the United States broke apart between Union and Confederacy, Daughters of Charity from Emmitsburg found themselves serving God in two countries split from one. In the United States, they were divided among New York, Massachusetts, Pennsylvania, Wisconsin,

Michigan, Illinois, Maryland and California. In the Confederate States, they served in Louisiana, Mississippi, Alabama, Missouri and Virginia.

About 300 Daughters of Charity were part of the 700 Catholic sisters who served in the Civil War primarily as nurses.

Though the Sisters and Daughters of Charity in the United States had been in existence for fifty-two years in 1861, their mother organization had been around since 1633. Saint Vincent de Paul, founder of the Daughters of Charity, told the sisters, "Men go to war to kill other men; and you, you go to war to repair the damage they do. What a blessing of God! Men kill the body-and very often the soul when those they kill die in mortal sin-and you go to restore life or, at least, to help to preserve it..."[4]

The Daughters of Charity in Europe had lived up to this mission and gained a reputation as battlefield nurses. During the Crimean War when England, France and Sardinia helped Turkey defend itself against Russia. The Daughters of Charity worked as nurses with the French soldiers, easing their pains and caring for the soldiers until they were healthy again.

The British quickly became dismayed at the conditions sick and wounded British soldiers were forced to endure. War correspondent Thomas Chenery had brought the plight of the British soldiers to light in his war reports and pointed out the excellent care the French received. He wrote in his newspaper report, "Why have we no Sisters of Charity?" It was a rallying call for better battlefield nursing care.[5]

Yet, even proper nursing care in hospitals at the time was still in its infancy. It was believed by many that nursing was not a suitable profession for women so nursing in public hospitals was often done by other residents of the hospital or the poor. No formal training program existed and most nurses either learned their skills by providing care to family members or assisting a doctor to whom they were related.

The Sisters of Charity of Emmitsburg entered into health care when they took over the management of nursing services of the Baltimore Infirmary in 1823 and five years later, they opened to the first Catholic hospital west of the Mississippi River.

The Sisters of Charity of Emmitsburg continued to grow. In 1850, when they affiliated themselves with the Mother House of the Daughters of Charity in Paris, they adopted the blue-grey dress, white collar and white cornette, they would eventually distinguish them as unique. They also adopted the name of their mother organization becoming Daughters, rather than Sisters, of Charity.

As the Civil War approached, the Daughters of Charity of Emmitsburg continued their work among the sick whoever they might be. They gained experience working with victims of violence, accidents and cholera in Baltimore, Philadelphia and Boston during outbreaks in 1832-1833 and 1850. The Daughters of Charity also cared for patients with yellow fever in the South during an 1855 outbreak.

The Baltimore Commissioners of Health report noted of the sisters:

> The zeal with which these important duties were performed, entitles those pious ladies to the highest praise from all humane persons, and has deeply impressed upon the members of this Board feelings of high respect, and obtained their most sincere thanks. [6]

These varied experiences in dangerous surroundings became the training ground for what they would face in the war. "What the prevailing opinion overlooked, however, was that sisters brought something to the battlefields that was rare: more nursing experience than the armies have,"[7] noted one modern historian who wrote of Sisternurses.

As the expectation of a war between the Union and Confederacy grew, it became obvious that the Daughters of Charity and some of the other Catholic sisterhoods were the only source for trained nurses to care for sick and wounded soldiers.

Professional nurses were virtually unheard of at the time. It was considered unladylike for women to care for men the way nurses needed to. Bathing men who weren't their husbands was something only women of ill repute would do. Male doctors worried that women would faint at the sight of the blood and gore.[8] Even in the army where care was needed more frequently, nursing care was generally done by other patients who were further along in their recovery.[9]

However, despite the reticence people had about the Catholic religion at the time, they showed little of that hesitation in accepting the care that the Daughters of Charity and other Catholic sisters offered. Mary Livermore, who worked with a sanitary commission during the war, wrote years later:

> I am neither a Catholic, nor an advocate of the monastic institutions of that church. Similar organizations established on the basis of the Protestant religion, and in harmony with republican principles, might be made very helpful to modern society, and would furnish occupation and give position to large numbers of unmarried women, whose hearts go out to the work in charitable intent. But I can never forget my experience during the War of Rebellion. Never did I meet these Catholic sisters in hospitals, on transports, on hospital steamers, without observing their devotion, faithfulness, and unobtrusiveness. They gave themselves no airs of superiority or holiness, shirked no duty, sought no easy place, bred no mischiefs. Sick and wounded men watched for their entrance into the wards at morning, and looked a regretful farewell when they departed at night. They broke down in exhaustion from overwork, as did the Protestant nurses; like them, they succumbed to the fatal prison-fever, which our exchanged pris-

oners brought from the fearful pens of the South.[10]

Such was the country broken and the Daughters of Charity of Emmitsburg would help heal it one body and one soul at a time.

Sister Mary Louise Caufield. Courtesy of the Daughters of Charity of St. Louise Archives, Emmitsburg, Md.

Care as an afterthought

Neither the Union nor the Confederacy was ready to care for those who survived the battles wounded and maimed at the start of the Civil War. The U.S. Army medical staff had only eighty-seven personnel. There had been the surgeon general, thirty surgeons and eighty-three assistant surgeons, but twenty-four of them had resigned their positions to return to their homes in the Confederate States and three others were discharged for disloyalty.

In the South, the Confederate Army had absorbed the state militias of the Confederate States, each of which had a surgeon and assistant surgeon among their members. As far as the number of medical personnel went, the Confederate Army had looked great compared to the Union Army. The problem was that most of the Confederate surgeons and assistant surgeons were not always fully trained, let alone surgeons who had experience treating war wounds.

Within two weeks of the beginning of the Civil War, 20,000-plus aid societies were established to help the soldiers and sailors who were protecting their country, be it Union or Confederate. Not all of the societies would continue for the full length of the war, but some would become very successful in their efforts.[11]

Recognizing the need to coordinate the efforts of the aid societies and manage the women volunteering to be nurses, U.S. Secretary of War Simon Cameron appointed Dorothea L. Dix, a Boston schoolteacher, as the superintendent of the U.S. Army nurses on April 23, 1861. Dix, who was a 60-year-old spinster, had earned a national reputation for two years of work in improving the conditions of the mentally ill. Cameron announced her service by writing:

> The free services of Miss D. L. Dix are accepted by the War Department and that she will give at all times all necessary and in organizing military hospitals for the cure of all sick and wounded soldiers, aiding the chief surgeon by supplying nurses and substantial means for the comfort and relief of the suffering; also that she is fully authorized to receive, control, and disburse special supplies bestowed by individuals or associations for the comfort of their friends or the citizen soldiers from all parts of the limited states; as also, under section of the Acting Surgeon-General, to draw from army stores.[12]

Dix took to her work immediately giving directions about supplies, equipment and operations. She traveled between the military hospitals to see what supplies each hospital had on hand. If a hospital was found lacking, she would fill out the supplies from the stores she kept in a house she rented.[13]

She also took steps to weed out women whom she thought would harm the reputation of her nurses. No woman under thirty-five years old need apply to serve in the government hospitals. All nurses were required to be healthy and plain-looking women. Their dresses had to be brown or black with no bows, no curls in their hair, no jewelry, and no hoop skirt.[14] But for these requirements, there may have been more women accepted as nurses. In fact, Mary Walker, a female Civil War doctor saw Dix turn away potential nurses, "telling them that they were too young and too good-looking and when they told her what their ages were she disputed their word and they left."[15] Nurse Jane Woolsey said, "Society just now presents the unprecedented spectacle of many women trying to make-believe that they are over thirty!"[16]

Though Dix's requirements would seem to fit many of the Catholic sisters and nuns serving in the war, Dix also had a "no Catholics need apply" proviso.[17]

One thing that may explain this proviso, other than the societal prejudice against Catholics, is that Dix had seen the charitable hospitals run by the Daughters of Charity in Paris in 1855 and come away less than overawed. She applauded the government support of the hospitals, but noted they had "two radical universal defects, at least."[18] These were poor ventilation and the experimental treatment methods used by the interns. She also expressed some distaste for the Catholic personnel at the hospital, writing:

> In *all* these establishments, associated with other employees, are found Sisters of Charity, and nuns of various orders. Some of them are very self-denying, not many. They are never overtasked, except possibly in some period of serious epidemic. As for the priests, they should for the most part occupy places in houses of correctional discipline, and enlightening cultivation.[19]

While Dix was less-than-impressed with the care the Sisters of Charity had offered, not everyone was impressed with Dix's work either. Dr. Mary Walker watched Dix tour a hospital once and wrote of her:

> When she saw a patient who was too ill to arrange the clothing on his cot if it became disarranged and a foot was

exposed she turned her head the other way seeming not to see the condition while I was so disgusted with such sham modesty that I hastened to arrange the soldier's bed clothing if I had a chance to be near when no nurses were to do this duty. I was not able to understand and am not to the present day of what use any one can be who professes to work for a cause and then allows sham modesty to prevent them from doing little services that chance to come their way.[20]

Another reason for Dix's opposition to Catholic involvement could have been her second goal, which was to bring all unregulated nursing activities throughout the country under her control.[21] However, in developing a nursing care system that met with her approval, Dix stepped on more than a few toes among officers, doctors and medical directors. Since the Catholic sisters were not under the jurisdiction of Dix, it made them an attractive alternative to use as nurses among men who didn't want to have to deal with Dix's demanding nature.

While Dix didn't want Catholic sisters helping with nursing, doctors on both sides of the fighting did. The Daughters of Charity work running hospitals and helping the sick during outbreaks of cholera and yellow fever in the previous decade were well known. It was also know that the Daughters of Charity were trained as nurses and not simply well-intentioned women.

Dix and her nurses were seen as stubborn and demanding by many doctors. Dr. John H. Brinton was the physician in charge at the Mound City Hospital at Mound City, Illinois. He wrote of his experience with Dix's nurses:

> On the arrival of certain trains they [the nurses] would stalk into the office of district commanders, and establish themselves solemnly against the walls, entrenched behind their bags and parcels. They defied all military law. There they were, and there they would stay, until some accommodation might be found for them.[22]

He noted that the nurses were usually sent to the adjutant general, who would in turn send the women to the physician in charge of the hospital, such as he was. Brinton wrote sarcastically, "They [the nurses] did not wish much, not they, simply a room, a bed, a looking glass, someone to get their meals and do little things for them, and they would nurse the sick boys of our gallant Union Army."[23]

Though it sounds as if he were against all women nurses, he wasn't. He only frowned on those who used up his hospital's scarce resources without providing a greater return for the wounded and sick soldiers. He found the nurses to be complainers, backbiters and fault finders. However, Brinton was pleased when fifteen Catholic sisters arrived to help and the Mother Superior told him that all they needed was single room for all the sisters.[24] Though Brinton doesn't say which Catholic sisterhood the women were from, he does note that the appeal for nurses was made to the Catholic authorities in South Bend, Indiana, so he may have been writing about the Sisters of the Holy Cross who were located in that city.

While Dix had been organizing her nurses, the Catholic sisters, the largest group of which was the Daughters of Charity of Emmitsburg, were already at work on the battlefields and in battlefield hospitals. During the civil war they served as nurses, hospital administrators, cooks, laundresses, dieticians and apothecaries.

Battlefield healthcare was as dangerous to a soldier's health as battle wounds. Around 60 percent of the casualties during the war came from infectious diseases like dysentery, typhus, malaria, smallpox, measles and tuberculosis because medicine at the time knew little about caring for infections.[25]

What would become quickly apparent is that the sisters brought more than physical relief to those they treated. Their patients recognized this even if the non-Catholics the sisters worked with didn't understand it.

Abby Hopper Gibbons was a Quaker who served as a nurse during the war. She wrote of a soldier at Point Lookout, Md., who told her, "Sisters, but they never enter into conversation with a soldier, and are, in consequence, but little comfort to the sick, while they work their machinery very well. All the sick are on our side."[26]

Either this was an isolated case or Hopper was expressing an anti-Catholic bias that she shared with much of the country at the time. The Daughters of Charity were women to whom sick and wounded soldiers could talk. Soldiers entrusted them with their hopes and fears.

Louisa May Alcott, the author of *Little Women*, served as a nurse in Washington City during the war. She described this effect, saying, "And now I knew that to him, as to so many, I was the poor substitute for mother, wife, or sister, and in his eyes no stranger, but a friend who hitherto had seemed neglectful."[27]

In the Missouri Military Hospital in St. Louis where the Daughters of Charity not only performed nursing duties but also administered the hospital, one sister wrote:

> Some of them looked upon the sisters as superior beings. They said they could not understand how persons could live in the world and not care for the world. One man expressed himself thus (and he was a non-Catholic) that the Daughters of Charity were like gold tried in the fire.[28]

Mother Ann Simeon. Courtesy of the Daughters of Charity of St. Louise Archives, Emmitsburg, Md.

To Gettysburg

Once the fighting at Gettysburg had ended, the Daughters of

34

Charity packed supplies to help with their northern neighbor. They were already providing battlefield nursing and hospital administration at many locations throughout both the Union and Confederacy. How could they not offer their help when the need was in their own backyard?

On Sunday, July 5, 1863, fourteen Daughters of Charity and Father Francis Burlando set out for Gettysburg in a carriage and omnibus, a journey of about nine miles. Because they had heard the sounds of the battle in Emmitsburg, they knew the wounded would need care that they could provide. They packed their carriage and omnibus with baskets of bandages, medicine and provisions and headed north. The journey was not without problems though.

> The Northern scouts were stationed here and there watching for the return of the Confederates. One of these bands seeing our carriage and omnibus and thinking that they were the ambulances of the enemy, were ready to fire on us. Later we reached a double blockade of zig-zag fence across the road. We wondered whether we dare go around it by turning into the fields, for in the distance we saw soldier, half hidden in the woods, watching us. Father Burlando tied his white handkerchief to his cane and holding it high, walked towards them while we also alighted and walked about so that they might see the cornettes. They viewed Father sharply, for they had resolved to refuse the Flag of Truce were it offered, but the cornette assured them that all was well.[29]

The soldiers lowered their weapons and moved the barrier – a line of tree stumps – across the road to the side so the carriage and omnibus could pass.

"As we passed, the pickets lifted their caps and bowed showing their pleasure on seeing the Sisters going up to attend the sufferers," Sister Matilda Coskery wrote.[30]

The small caravan came upon the battlefield suddenly and they were shocked. Father Burlando wrote:

> What a frightful spectacle met our gaze! Houses burnt, dead bodies of both Armies strewn here and there, an immense number of slain horses, thousands of bayonets, sabres,

wagons, wheels, projectiles of all dimensions, blankets, caps, clothing of every color covered the woods and fields. We were compelled to drive very cautiously to avoid passing over the dead. Our terrified horses drew back or darted forward reeling from one side to the other. The farther we advanced the more harrowing was the scene; we could not restrain our tears.[31]

Sister Matilda wrote a more-heart-wrenching account.

But on reaching the Battle grounds, awful! to see men lying dead on the road some by the side of their horses. – O, it was beyond description – hundreds of both armies lying dead almost on the track that the driver had to be careful not to pass over the bodies – O! this picture of human beings slaughtered down by their fellow men in a cruel civil war was perfectly awful. The battlefield a very extensive space on either side of the road – the east was Meads (sic) stand the west Lonstreet's (sic) on both sides were men diging (sic) pits and putting the bodies down by the dozens. One newly made grave contained fifty bodies of Confederates. -- …in another spot might be pointed out where the body of such a Genl lay until removed to another location – in this frightful condition we found the Battlegrounds of that fearful Battle of Gettysburg.[32]

The group also watched the bands of soldiers assigned to digging the mass graves for the fallen. There seemed to be no order to their work. Where the bodies lay, holes were dug to bury the men. If bodies were numerous, large holes were dug for mass graves. At Culp's Hill, the sisters saw sixty Confederate soldiers buried in one trench.

Confusion still reigned in the town of Gettysburg as well. One member of the group wrote:

At last we reached the city of Gettysburg. Here a large portion of the Army was guarding the battlefield. All the avenues and environs of the city were encumbered with soldiers, horses, wagons, and artillery carts. The inhabitants were just emerging from the cellars to which they had fled for safety during the combat; terror was depicted on every countenance; all was confusion. Every house, every temple, the courthouse, the Protestant Seminary, the Catholic Church-all were filled with the wounded; and yet, there were thousands still stretched on the battlefield with scarcely any assistance, it being impossible to provide for all.[33]

The group moved slowly through the muddy streets and crowds of people. They stopped at McClellan's Hotel on the downtown square in the center of Gettysburg. The hotel not only had guest rooms but large common rooms that would soon be filled with the wounded from the battlefield.

Our little band of Sisters was disposed of by sending two to each hospital as far as their number went. Our headquarters were the parlors of McClennans Hotel which had been set aside exclusively for the Sisters' use. All of the churches were filled with the wounded; the Blessed Sacrament had been removed from the Catholic Church and even its sanctuary was filled with some of the worst cases, especially men whose limbs had been amputated. Because we had to make our way to the town at a snail's pace it was one o'clock in the afternoon before our real work began but after that the Sisters labored heroically and without respite.[34]

The arrival of the sisters at St. Francis Xavier Catholic Church allowed the medical personnel there to assist hundreds of wounded soldiers. So many wounded were in the church that the sisters could barely pass between them. Indeed, every large building in Gettysburg had become a hospital, in all more than 113 of them.[35]

Father Burlando heard some confessions and then returned to Emmitsburg. The sisters returned to McClellan's Hotel late that evening. Father Burlando wrote later:

After making our first round to the sick and wounded we returned to the Hotel and took some refreshment, then we were off again to our patients. The weather was warm and damp as is usually the case where a large quantity of gunpowder has been used. We did not see a woman that evening. The feminine element had either escaped to the country or remained hidden in the cellars. The next day the women appeared in their homes and looked like frightened ghosts, so terrified had they been during the fearful battle, and no wonder! The Sisters lay on the floor that night and needless to say they did not sleep very much. On the following day Mother Ann Simeon sent us beds, bed-covering, cooked ham, coffee, tea, and whatever she thought the Sisters actually needed. Sister Euphemia, the Assistant, had gone to attend to the Sisters in the Confederate Military Hospital, which, though it was a source of comfort to the poor Sisters in the South, increased the labor of Mother Ann Simeon. On the second day a reinforcement of Sisters from Baltimore came to our aid.[36]

Though Father Burlando had work to do in Emmitsburg, he continued to visit the sisters at Gettysburg. Returning home each night having seen the horrors left behind on the battlefield, Father Burlando was troubled by visions of what he had seen. Even as he sat down to write his superior in France three days after his first visit to the battlefield, he could hear cannon fire to the Southwest and where such sounds could be heard death was sure to follow. He wrote:

My God when will you give peace to our unhappy country! We well merit these frightful chastisements, and they will not cease until we shall have been well humiliated. Aid us with your prayers, because the American does not pray; -- and yet, without prayer how shall we appease the anger of God?[37]

Father Burlando realized that more help would be needed, but finding it among the Daughters of Charity of Emmitsburg was difficult. Many sisters were working at other hospitals in other states and were needed just as much there as they were at Gettysburg. In addition, the Daughters of Charity were still operating schools across the country.

He returned the following day with more sisters to give aid as well as beds and blankets for the sisters.

Father James Francis Burlando was the spiritual director for the American Daughters of Charity during the Civil War. Courtesy of the Daughters of Charity of St. Louise Archives, Emmitsburg, Md.

The additional help came from sisters who arrived from Baltimore and it was much-needed. Of the 650 doctors with the Union Army, 544 of them went with the army in the pursuit of General Lee at the end of the battle.[38]

As the Daughters of Charity went about their work, ambulances were provided to carry clothing, supplies, etc. to the wounded. Sister Camilla O'Keefe wrote, "Hundreds of poor fellows lay on the ground with only their blankets under them; they were delighted when they could secure a little straw brought from some neighboring farm by a friendly hand."[39]

One sister was seen using a teaspoon to give a drink to a dying man. It was slow work for a man who would soon die from his injuries, but she was able to bring him comfort in his final hours.

The sisters would carry the horrible sights of the battlefield with them. The ground appeared plowed by the shells of the battle. Though many of the bodies had been removed to hospitals, others still remained exposed to the elements. And even where there weren't bodies, there was evidence that they had been there – knapsacks, bayonet sheaths and weapons strewn around.

The Daughters of Charity searched for wounded daily. At one point, they saw a red flag on the battlefield that stood in the ground next to a sign that read: "1700 wounded down this way." The sisters diverted in that direction until they found the wounded. Mother Ann Simeon wrote:

> O, yes for some were in a frightful condition. The Sister too brought plenty of the vermin along on their clothes! – I shudder on thinking of this part of the Sisters sufferings. … The weather was very warm. We noticed one large man whose leg had to be taken off another part of his body was in such a condition that the big maggots were crawling on the ground on which they crept from the body. Many others almost as bad but the whole of them were crawling with *lice* so that the Sisters did a great deal for those poor fellows by getting *combs* to get their heads clear of the troublesome *animals*.[40]

In an unusual incident, two Daughters of Charity—Sister Mary Veronica Klimkiewicz and Sister Serena Klimkiewicz—were providing care to the wounded soldiers on the battlefield. Sister Veronica was working amid death and carnage when she was given a very pleasant surprise.

> Going over a field encampment we found the brother of one of our Sisters who was in a hospital in the town. He had been wounded in the chest and in the ankle. The kind officer allowed him to be removed to the hospital where is Sister was stationed. They had not seen each other for nine years.[41]

Sister Camilla O'Keefe. Courtesy of the Daughters of Charity of St. Louise Archive, Emmitsburg, Md.

Nursing at Gettysburg

The sisters' work in treating the wounded at Gettysburg lasted for weeks. Three sisters spent their time working at one field hospital until all of the wounded could be moved to regular hospitals in New York or Philadelphia where more Daughters of Charity usually wound up caring for them.

Though the sisters' primary goal was to help soldiers recover physically, the care also gave them a chance to break down barriers. "This section of the country knew nothing of the holiness of Catholicity but believed much that was untrue. We expected to encounter some difficulty on that score but to our surprise all who met us lauded our charity. Bitterness had lost its edge and modesty might blush at the welcome and heartfelt greetings that met us everywhere," Mother

Ann Simeon wrote.[42]

In one instance an "elderly gentleman" came to Gettysburg short-ly after the fighting ending looking for his son. While he knew his son had been in the fighting, he had no idea of whether his son survived. While the man was sitting on a bench outside of the McClellan's Ho-tel, a group of sisters arrived with clothing for the wounded.

"Good God! Can those sisters be the persons whose religion we always run down!" the man said.

The hotel owner William McClellan told him, "Yes, they are the very persons who are run down by those who know nothing of their charity."[43]

McClellan told the man that many people were having the same reaction and that "some of them fairly swore that they would never again believe anything wrong of persons who would do what the Sis-ters had been doing on the battlefield of Gettysburg."[44]

The success of the Daughters of Charity in caring for the wound-ed also earned them more respect from the doctors they worked with. Upon arrival at one hospital, the surgeon in charge took the sisters to meet the other female volunteers.

"Ladies, and you, men and nurses also, here are the Sisters of Charity who have come to serve our men. They will give all the direc-tions here. You are only required to observe them," the surgeon told them.[45]

Amid the carnage, the Daughters of Charity who nursed soldiers at the hospital established in the Methodist church in Gettysburg ac-tually found amusement when they went to the commissaries for clothing and other necessaries. The person in charge of the commis-sary would see their religious attire and say, "Sisters, I suppose you want them for the Catholic church hospital."

"No," the sisters would say, "We want them for the Methodist church hospital."[46]

While at Gettysburg, Dr. A. B. Stonelake came to the hotel where the sisters were staying and inquired if any of the sisters who had served at Point Lookout were in the area. One of the sisters was near-by and Dr. Stonelake walked over to meet her and Father Burlando. The doctor had worked with the Daughters of Charity in Hammond Hospital at Point Lookout. He had been so impressed by their service and humility that he had been baptized into the Catholic Church.

The doctor accompanied the sisters into the field to help care for the wounded. Sister Camilla O'Keefe wrote of him:

> This good physician not only performed the duties of his profession but after he had set and bandaged shattered limbs, he worked like a common carpenter. From a farmhouse he obtained a saw, an axe, some stray board and some nails, and in a short time he had the men whom we found lying on the ground, raised on a kind of frame which made the poor sufferers feel that they were in beds.[47]

Most of the prisoners whom the sisters were helping were from Georgia and Alabama and knew little of religion. They hadn't been baptized, which was fine, since many of them didn't even believe in Heaven or Hell.[48] So Dr. Stonelake took the time to talk to the prisoners and testify to them of his own religious experiences.

Some of the soldiers listened and began making connections, saying, "The Sisters are Catholics, and surely they must be right."[49]

Before long, fifty of the men, some of them Confederate officers, converted and were baptized. The wounded had been taken to the Catholic church in town and they recovered under pictures of the Stations of the Cross hanging around on the walls, and a very large painting of Saint Francis Xavier holding up a crucifix to show the benighted pagans the sign of our Redemption.

> The men lay on the seats of the pews, under the pews, in every aisle; in the gallery and in the sanctuary there was hardly room to pass between them. Their own blood, the water used for bathing their wounds, all kinds of filth and stench added to their misery. The very air was vitiated by the odor of gangrenous wounds but there was never a complaint from these heroic men. A considerable number of them were dying from lockjaw, and this demanded much time for giving drinks and nourishment.[50]

With few surgeons available, for many men, their first medical treatment came from the kind words of the Daughters of Charity.

One sister found a tall Scotsman lying under a pew with only his head visible. He suffered from lockjaw, a bacterial infection of an open wound that attacks the nervous system and causes spasms in the jaw and facial muscles. He was close to dying. The lockjaw had spread to other areas of the body and threatened to stop his breathing. Because the Scotsman had never been baptized, the sister sat with him and talked of God and the church.

A crowd soon began gathering to listen.

The Scotsman was too ill to be moved and so he was baptized where he lay, shortly before his death.[51]

In another instance, a young cavalry officer saw one of these impromptu baptisms of a nearby soldier. The soldier asked the priest to baptism him and the priest obliged him.

The soldier awoke the next morning and asked a sister, "Will Jack die?"

The soldier was referring to his horse, which had been injured in the battle. The sister didn't realize this and answered, "No."

"Will I die?"

"I think so," the sister answered quietly.

The honest admission upset the soldier more than the pain from his wounds did. The sister tried to calm him, but his anxiety only grew more agitated. In particular, he worried over his fear of receiving judgment for his life and that he had no religion.

"My poor brother, did you not receive baptism yesterday?" the sister asked.

"Yes, but I should feel religion."

The sister spoke to him of God's love in a quiet and soothing voice. The man relaxed and then smiled as his soul found itself at ease.

"I do believe I have religion," he finally told the sister.

The earnest soldier was still at peace when he died.[52]

The sisters didn't convince everyone, though. Another young soldier chose not be baptized in the face of death. A surgeon told one of the Daughters of Charity that she should baptize the soldier anyway. However, the sister honored the soldier's wishes. She was there to serve and not to force her religion on anyone.

When the soldier's father arrived to visit his son, the sister told the father that his son didn't seem worried about not being baptized.

"Oh, no," the father said. "My Lou is a good boy. He volunteered in his country's service, fought her battles, dies for her and that will do."

"Surely you are baptized?" the sister asked.

"Yes, but my son does not need it."

So when the young soldier died, his father took his unbaptized body home for burial.[53]

St. Joseph College in Emmitsburg during the Civil War. This was where the mother house for the American Daughters of Charity was located. Courtesy of the Library of Congress.

Four Daughters of Charity were assigned to care for the wounded at Pennsylvania College,[54] which had been converted into a hospital housing 600 men. Some of the worst cases were sent here.

With a scarcity of surgeons, the sisters could only dress the wounds of the soldiers and try to ease their pain through their careful ministrations. "Every morning when they returned, eight or ten dead bodies lay at the entrance of the college awaiting interment."[55]

Amid this carnage, the sisters brought so many men to baptism that they lost count. "Very rarely did any one in danger refuse baptism when we could give the time for it, but to hear the men call piteously, 'Come to me when you have finished with his wounds,' obliged us to do violence to every other duty," one sister wrote.[56]

So many wounded were brought to the college that some of them had to be housed outdoors. In one instance, two young soldiers lay on a blanket with a little trench about two inches deep dug around them to direct the rain runoff so that they lay in the mud rather than a pool of water.

Another time, a sister heard a commotion among the patients in the college hospital wards. She saw a group of men with guns pointed at a man. With no one else stepping in to help, the sister walked over to the group and put her hand on the man who seemed about to be shot. She pushed back the door of the surgeon's room and led the man through it while holding out her other arm to prevent the armed men from following.

Without saying a word, the men lowered their weapons and left.

A doctor came over to her and said, "Sister, you have surprised me! I shall never, never forget what I have just witnessed. I saw the men's anger and all the excitement, but I feared my presence would only increase it. I did not know what to do, when you came and made everything right."

"Well," said the sister, "what more did I do than anyone else would have done? You know they would be ashamed to resist a female."

"A female!" exclaimed the doctor, "All the women of Gettysburg could not effect what you have done. No, no one but a Sister of Charity could have done this. Truly, it would have been well, if a company of Sisters of Charity could have been in the War, for then it would not have continued for four years. The Sisters can do what they please. I shall never forget this scene."[57]

Another soldier refused a sister's kindnesses, possibly due to the bias and intolerance toward Catholics at the time. The sister persevered and the man finally began to respond to her kindness.

When the sister found out that the man was in danger of dying from his wounds, she broached the subject of baptism. He said he was too old to worry about baptism. After making no progress with him for two weeks, the sister removed the miraculous medal from her chaplet and slipped it under the soldier's pillow while he was sleeping.

"Blessed Mother, I can do no more for this man," the sister said to herself. "I leave him to you."

The next morning when the sister visited the man, he asked for a drink and then told her, "Sister, I do not want any breakfast today, but I want to be baptized."

She told him that he needed to feel sorrow for his sins.

"I have cried over them all night and also for my obstinacy towards your kindness. Will you please forgive me?" the man asked.

The sister easily forgave him. She had just baptized him when he died.[58]

Though the Daughters of Charity were happy to see the ranks of

American Catholics growing, they did not prohibit or work against other religious representatives from baptizing soldiers.

One young man worried that he couldn't be immersed in the waters of baptism because he was crippled.

The Nuns of the Battlefield Memorial in Washington, D.C. was dedicated in 1924 to all of the Catholic sisters who served in the Civil War. Courtesy of the Library of Congress.

"Sister, it is very strange that no one says baptism is so necessary but you sisters," the man said.

A nearby Protestant minister heard the soldier and said, "Yes, young man, I say baptism is necessary and I am a minister. If you desire it, I will baptize you."

The soldier considered this and said, "Well, if you do it as Sister would, you may, but Sister, I want you to stay right here and see that he does it right."

The minister explained how he baptized people. The soldier asked the sister if that was the correct way and she nodded that it was, and so, the minister baptized the soldier.

The soldier asked the sister to remain with him as he died and he prayed until his last breath. His final words were, "O Lord, bless all the Sisters of Charity."[59]

In another instance, a soldier noticed a sister giving a medal to Catholic soldier.

"Sister, you gave something to that man a while ago and he must be easier for he has not groaned since. Please give me what you gave him," the soldier asked because he was suffering from his own pains.

The sister did and told the soldier about what the medal represented and a prayer he should say.

Later, the soldier told her, "I do not long to live except to help my parents; the doctor says I can be saved only by the amputation of my limb. I cannot bear this."

The sister talked to the doctor about the young soldier and was told that his only chance at life lay in amputating his limb. The doctor worried that it might already be too late to save the soldier's life if an infection or gangrene had set in.

The sister begged the soldier to submit to the operation for his own sake.

"Well, baptize me first, and then promise me that the doctors will not take the medal off my neck," the soldier said.

Worried that the soldier might die, the sister baptized the soldier and told him he could keep the medal. The soldier agreed to the operation but refused anesthetic during his operation. Instead he kept the medal where he could see it.

Despite the pain of the operation, he murmured only twice. He said, "O, my mother, my mother!"

The soldier survived the operation and while he was recovered, the sister sent someone to teach him about the Catholic church.

Once the soldier was able to move around, he would often point to the sister and say to anyone who would listen, "There is the Sister who saved my body and soul."[60]

On November 19, President Abraham Lincoln visited Gettysburg for the dedication of the Soldiers' National Cemetery. Though he was not featured speaker, his short remarks would be the ones remembered as "The Gettysburg Address." By then the Daughters of Charity of Emmitsburg had moved on to care for soldiers in other hospitals and battlefields throughout the country in the hopes that their care would keep places like Soldiers' National Cemetery from swelling in numbers.

[1] CWSAC Battle Summaries: Gettysburg, *www.nps.gov/history/hps/abpp/battles/pa002.htm*

[2] Daughters of Charity, *Mother Regina Smith and Mother Ann Simeon* (Emmitsburg, MD: St. Joseph's, 1939) p. 129. Hereafter cited as *Mother Ann Simeon.*

[3] William Barnaby Faherty, *Exile in Erin: a Confederate chaplain's story : the life of Father John B. Bannon* (St. Louis, MO: Missouri History Museum 2002) p. 77.

[4] Vincent de Paul, translated by Sister Marie Poole. "Trust in Divine Providence (Common Rules, Art 41)." Conference of June 9, 1658. CCD volume 10, p. 407.

[5] *Times of London*, October 14, 1854.

[6] T. Sheppard, Jacob Deems and Peter Foy. *Report of the Commissioners of Health*, Baltimore City Health Department, 1815-1849. 1832. Maryland State Archives (Baltimore, MD).

[7] John J. Fialka, *Sisters: Catholic Nuns and the Making of America* (New York, NY: Macmillan, 2004) p. 61.

[8] Sister Mary Denis Maher, *To Bind the Wounds: Catholic Sister Nurses in the U.S. Civil War* (Baton Rouge, LA: LSU Press, 1999) pp. 38-39.

[9] Frank R. Freemon, *Gangrene and Glory: Medical Care During the American Civil War* (Urbana, IL: University of Illinois Press, 2001) p. 52.

[10] Mary Livermore, *What Shall We Tell Our Daughters: Superfluous Women and Other Lectures* (Boston, MA: Lee and Shepard, 1883) pp. 177-178.

[11] Mary Massey, *Bonnet Brigades: American Woman and the Civil War* (New York: Knopf, 1966) p. 32.

[12] U.S. War Department, *The War of the Rebellion: A Compilation of the Official Records of the Union and Confederate Armies* (Washington, D.C.: U.S. Government Printing Office, 1880-1901), Series III, Part I, p. 107.

[13] George Worthington Adams, *Doctors in Blue, The Medical History of the Union Army in the Civil War* (New York, NY: Henry Schuman, 1952) p. 179.

[14] Dorothea Dix. *Circular No. 8.* Washington, D.C. July 14, 1862.

[15] Agatha Young, *The Women and the Crisis: Women of the North in the Civil War* (New York, NY: McDowell, Oblesky, 1959) p. 99.

[16] Jane Stuart Woolsey, *Hospital Days, Reminiscence of a Civil War Nurse* (Roseville, MN: Edinborough Press, 1996) p. 4.

[17] Jeane Heimberger Candido, "Sisters and Nuns Who Were Nurses During the Civil War," *Blue and Gray Magazine*, October 1993.

[18] Francis Tiffany, *Life of Dorothea Lynde Dix* (New York, NY: Houghton Mifflin Company, 1918) p. 282-283.

[19] Tiffany, p. 282-283.

[20] Dorris Moore Lawson, *Dr. Mary E. Walker: A Biographical Sketch*, Master's Thesis, (Syracuse, NY: Syracuse University, 1954) p. 39.

[21] Agatha Young, *The Women and the Crisis: Women of the North in the Civil War* (New York, NY: McDowell, Obolensky, 1959) p. 98.

[22] John H. Brinton, *Personal Memoirs of John H. Brinton: Major and Surgeon, U.S.V.,* 1861-1865 (New York, NY: Neale Publishing Co., 1914) pp. 43-44.

[23] Brinton, p. 44.

[24] Brinton, pp. 44-45.

[25] Fialka, p. 62.

[26] Sarah Hopper Emerson, ed., *Abby Hopper Gibbons: Told Chiefly Through Her Correspondence, vol. II* (New York, NY: The Knickerbocker Press, 1896) p. 32.

[27] *Annals of the Civil War*, APSL (formerly ASJPH), pp. 478-81. Note: This is a collection of first-person accounts of sisters' war-time experiences submitted by the Daughters of Charity following the war at the request of Father Francis Burlando.

[28] Betty Ann McNeil, D.C., *Dear Masters: Extracts from Accounts by Sister Nurses* (Emmitsburg, MD: Daughters of Charity Emmitsburg Province, 2011) p. 77.

[29] *Mother Ann Simeon*, p. 130.

[30] *Annals*, pp. 535, 561.

[31] Father Burlando, C.M. letter to Rev. Jean-Baptiste Etienne, C. M. as quoted in Elin Kelly, *Numerous Choirs: A Chronicle of Elizabeth Bayley Seton and Her Spiritual Daughters* (Evansville, 1996), p. 235.

[32] *Annals, vol. I,* p. 536.

[33] *Annals, vol. I,* p. 562.

[34] *Mother Ann Simeon, p. 131.* Note: The quote incorrectly named McClellan's Hotel as McClennans.

[35] *Provincial Annals (1846-1871),* APSL (formerly ASJPH), pp. 537-538.

[36] *Mother Ann Simeon*, p. 131.

[37] *Annals, vol. I,* pp. 562-563.

[38] Jonathan Letterman, "Report on the Operations of the Medical Department during the Battle of Gettysburg." *MSH, Medical Volume, pt. 1*, appendix, pp.140-2.

[39] *Mother Ann Simeon*, p. 132; Betty Ann McNeil, *Charity Afire Civil War Trilogy: Pennsylvania* (Emmitsburg, MD: Daughters of Charity Emmitsburg Province, 2011), p. 3.

[40] *Annals, vol. I,* pp. 539-540.

[41] Sister M. Liguori, H.F.N. "Polish Sisters in the Civil War," *Polish American Studies* 7:1-2 (1950).

[42] *Mother Ann Simeon*, p. 133.

[43] *Mother Ann Simeon*, pp. 133-134.

[44] *Mother Ann Simeon*, p. 134.

[45] *Mother Ann Simeon*, p. 134.

[46] Loyola Law and Betty Ann McNeil, *Daughters of Charity in the Civil War: Extracts from Personal Accounts of Sister Nurses* (2002 manuscript) p. 71.

[47] *Mother Ann Simeon*, p. 135; McNeil, *Pennsylvania*, p. 4.

[48] *Mother Ann Simeon*, p. 135.

[49] *Mother Ann Simeon*, p. 135.

[50] *Mother Ann Simeon*, p. 136-137.

[51] *Mother Ann Simeon*, p. 137.

[52] *Mother Ann Simeon*, pp. 137-138.

[53] *Mother Ann Simeon*, p. 138.

[54] Pennsylvania College became Gettysburg College in 1921.

[55] George Barton, *Angels of the Battlefield: A History of the Labors of the Catholic Sisterhoods in the Late Civil War* (Philadelphia, PA: The Catholic Art Publishing Company, 1897) pp. 98.

[56] *Mother Ann Simeon*, p. 139.

[57] *Mother Ann Simeon*, pp. 139-140.

[58] *Mother Ann Simeon*, p. 140.

[59] *Mother Ann Simeon*, pp. 140-141.

[60] *Mother Ann Simeon*, p. 141-142.

8

Demi-Gods Walked Among Gettysburg College Students

Gettysburg College has boasted many notable alumni including athletes, businessmen, military officers and…demigods.

At the turn of the century, the Sons of Hercules were the stars of Gettysburg College. Hercules was a Roman demi-god. His father was Zeus, king of the gods, and the mortal Alcmene. Hercules was famous for his strength and great feats he accomplished performing his famous "12 Labors of Hercules."

The Sons of Hercules formed in 1893. They were a group of 15 to 20 students who are commonly called gymnasts nowadays, but in their time, they were so much more.

The Sons of Hercules performed in an annual exhibition in either February or March. It was the result of months of training from the beginning of the school year in the previous fall. Interested men would try out for the team and eventually the numbers were winnowed down.

In 1898, *The Gettysburgian* noted, "The exhibitions given by the "Sons" are always interesting. Besides the regular drills they give exhibitions of club swinging, trapeze work, parallel bars, tumbling, pyramid building, specialties in several lines, fencing, boxing, and wrestling."

During the 1898 exhibition, the old gymnasium was packed with spectators. The Gettysburgian noted that the five rows of seats that had been set up surrounding the gymnasium floor and above the floor on the running track. The crowd that attended the 1899 exhibition was the largest ever gathered in the gym, according to *The Gettysburgian.*

The exhibition began with a musical performance from the mandolin club. Then came the first feats of the Sons of the Hercules as they showed their mat work followed by their work on the horizontal bar. Two sons then demonstrated their hand-eye coordination with the Indian clubs. The mandolin club performed again followed by the Sons of Hercules demonstrating their skills on the pommel horse and building human pyramids. After a performance from the glee club, the sophomore and freshman classes faced off in a basketball game. At the half time break, two Sons of Hercules pummeled each other in a boxing match. The exhibition ended with the second half of the basketball game.

The Sons of Hercules pose for their team photo. Courtesy of Special Collections/Musselman Library, Gettysburg College.

"Every event was performed in good shape, many of the men astonishing the crowd with their exhibitions of agility and strength," *The Gettysburgian* reported.

The newspaper noted not only the strength involved in the feats but how graceful the men looked performing them.

"While the musical clubs added variety to the entertainment, the greatest success of the evening was Bickel, '02, as clown. Being himself a member of the team, he could follow them through every event, and kept the audience in perpetual merriment by his sallies. This feature is one that should not be forgotten in future exhibitions," *The Gettysburgian* reported.

The club was also very generous with its proceeds from admission to the exhibition. The Sons of Hercules donated portions of their profits to help the college athletic association, the mandolin club and the college track fund.

The team called themselves "The Sons of Hercules" until the end of the 1902-1903 school year. The following year, the Sons of Hercules added "Gymnasium Team" to its name and then in the 1904-1905 and the following two years, they were simply called the Gymnasium Team.

9

GETTYSBURG'S FIRST ATTEMPT AT A PUBLIC LIBRARY

History books point to 1946 as the opening of the first public library in Adams County. However, a version of the public library could be found in Gettysburg even earlier in 1895.

In the mid-1890's, the Gettysburg YMCA started an effort to open a reading room for residents staying there. Books were solicited and a collection started, but the effort fell through before the reading room opened, according to the *Gettysburg Compiler*.

The question then became what should be done with the books that had been collected for the reading room.

In May 1894, Charles M. McCurdy, E. S. Breidenbaugh and J. W. Richard formed the Gettysburg Free Reading Room and Library Association. The *Compiler* published the association's articles of agreement on May 15. In addition to offering a place where anyone could come and read books, magazines and newspapers, two of the stated goals of the association were that the free public reading room would be a place:

- Where familiar talks on practical subjects may be made to young men by home and other talent.
- Where good influences may be brought to bear upon young men in every possible way.

Association members would solicit money and donations for the reading room and help maintain it. A person could become a member by paying the annual $2 dues, which would go toward paying rent for the room and buying materials to read.

Elsie Singmaster Lewars stands in front of the first Adams County Public Library at 135 Carlisle Street in Gettysburg. Courtesy of the Adams County Public Library.

On March 19, 1895, the free public reading room opened in Gettysburg. A reading room is similar to a library except that the items must remain on site and must be read in the reading room. They are not loaned out to be taken home. To introduce the public to the "uses and benefits of reading and public reading rooms", separate meetings were held for men and women on the opening day.

"Gettysburg's citizens ought to give their support to the Public Reading Room opened last week. It has been organized by the private efforts of a few gentlemen who are interested in the good of the town," the *Compiler* proclaimed.

The newspaper was a big supporter of the free public reading room. The March 26, 1895, edition noted that a scholarly paper had been written recently that said Pennsylvania was the only northern state that had not adopted a law permitting communities to tax themselves for the support of free libraries.

"Gettysburg has been destitute of a place of this kind for many years, if indeed, we ever had a public reading place," the *Compiler* wrote.

While the newspaper praised those people who had magazine and newspaper subscriptions and a library of books, it noted that they should also support the reading room to allow others the same opportunities.

The Gettysburg Free Public Reading Room failed to get enough support to continue and folded after a short time with a debt and a library of materials.

In 1890, the *Compiler* reported, "For the purpose of partially liquidating this indebtedness, all of which is now paid, it was proposed by one of the gentlemen of the committee that he would give a reasonable consideration for these books and would transfer them to the High School. This was looked upon as being altogether the right disposition to make of this public property, and the arrangements were consummated."

Thus ended Gettysburg's first experiment with a free public library.

It wasn't the only effort to promote reading in the county. The Berlin Improvement Society had a small library of 600 books in 1836 that were exchanged among its members. Some schools also had small libraries. With these libraries, though, you had to be a society member or a student at the school to use the books. The Gettysburg Free Public Reading Room had been just what its name said: free and open to the public.

Efforts to start a free public library didn't resume in Adams County until 1931 when the Gettysburg Chamber of Commerce began urging the county commissioners to contribute $3,500 annually to support a public library. Finally in November 1944, Elsie Singmaster Lewars, O.H. Benson, John Knickerbocker, Mrs. Lester O. Johnson and others formed the Adams County Free Library Association.

The association attracted 3,000 members who worked to open a library for Adams County.

"Thus encouraged, they rented quarters at 135 Carlisle Street in Gettysburg and in 1946 opened Adams County's first public library," Robert Bloom wrote *in A History of Adams County, Pennsylvania 1700-1900.*

10

THE SECOND BATTLE OF GETTYSBURG BEGINS

In 2005, the U.S. Supreme Court decided in the case of Kelo v. City of New London that government could use eminent domain not just to claim property for the public good but to actually take it from one private owner and give it to another private owner for the public good. In the Kelo case, property was taken from its owner and given to a private developer on the promise of redevelopment benefits to the community. To date, the property still hasn't been redeveloped.

You may wonder what this has to do with Gettysburg history. Well, if wasn't for the time that Gettysburg had a case before the Supreme Court, the Kelo case might have been decided differently.

The Gettysburg Electric Railway was incorporated in July 1892. The idea was for the trolley system to not only carry people throughout Gettysburg but to also take tourists out onto the battlefield. A Philadelphia newspaper reported that the route "will start from the square in Gettysburg, run out the Baltimore Pike, pass Cemetery Hill, encircle the National Cemetery, thence along the Emmittsburg Rd. to the Peach Orchard, through the Wheatfield to Devil's Den, and through the Valley of Death to Little Round Top Park. The return will be made via the Bloody Angle and Hancock Avenue to Gettysburg."

As part of the construction, a group of Italian workmen from Baltimore began blasting on William Tipton's land that contained Devil's Den. The explosions were loud enough to be heard in Gettysburg.

One eyewitness wrote, "All along the line, in the vicinity of Devil's Den, there is heavy blasting and digging and filling; and great havoc is played with the landscape. Huge masses of rock are displaced, great boulders are moved, the valley is to be filled the width and height of a track from the bridge over Plum Run in front of Round Top to the north end of the Valley and a whole new appearance will be given to the famous field of carnage," according to Nancy Householder on the Gettysburg Discussion Group .

As the 30-foot-wide path was cut through the historic site, veterans and some citizens grew more and more worried that a national landmark would be lost.

"Historic trees were felled, streams were forded, and rocks that still should the scars of battle were forever blasted from the face of the earth. In some instances' the trolley roadbed passed within feet of monuments that had been dedicated just a few years before. Public outcry was immediate and in some cases very bitter," Householder wrote.

John Bachelder came to Gettysburg in June 1893 to see the situation first hand and make a preliminary report to the U.S. Secretary of War. He wrote, in part, "The boulders which covered the combatants in the desperate engagement between the Fourth Maine and the 44th New York of the Union Army and the 44th Alabama and the right of Bennings Brigade of the Confederate army are already blasted, and the fragments broken under the hammer and are covered with earth to form a roadbed. And it is this locality which has been turned into a park to which cheap excursions are to be run from Baltimore and other cities. This is the most wild and picturesque section of the field. For the distance of over one mile before reaching this locality, the road cuts ruthlessly through the scene of some of the most desperate encounters of the battle."

Though the opponents to the trolley could do little to stop construction because the track was being laid on private lands, that benefit soon turned against the Gettysburg Electric Railway and brought progress to halt. The 72nd Pennsylvania Infantry Regiment owned a tract of land at The Angle that the railway needed to cross. The regiment refused to grant the railway a right of way. Because of this, the Gettysburg Electric Railway Company was forced to use a portion of the Gettysburg and Harrisburg Railroad to run along the Emmitsburg Road.

And so began the second Battle of Gettysburg.

The federal government begins taking over the battlefield

The Gettysburg Electric Railway started laying its tracks through the Gettysburg Battlefield in 1892. In some cases, the battlefield itself was altered to make way for the track.

This did not sit well with veterans and citizens who sought to pre-serve the battlefield as it had been in 1863.

"The idea of the Nation acquiring an entire battlefield and pre-serving it for historical purposes was new in 1890. It is therefore not surprising that it soon engendered a serious controversy, which arose, fittingly enough, at Gettysburg," Ronald F. Lee wrote in *The origins & evolution of the national park idea.*

The Gettysburg Trolley running near Devil's Den. Courtesy of the Adams County Historical Society.

Tensions between supporters and opponents of the Gettysburg Trolley rose with each explosion and felled tree. In 1893, 40 people asked the Pennsylvania Attorney General to step in and stop the trol-ley, but it was countered by a petition signed by 326 people in favor of the trolley.

Attorney General William Hensel refused to step in. He wrote, in part, "the right of owners of private property—whatever public inter-est may attach to it—to dispose of it to passenger railway corpora-tions, cannot be disputed. ...the line itself...has been chosen with a view of affording tourists the best possible means of visiting and viewing this great battlefield and doing the least possible injury to its natural conditions."

While trolley line construction did halt in August 1893 because of a lack of funds, operations did begin in September as far as the tracks did run at that point. However, the company was insolvent and went into receivership. The trolley continued operating, though, and track laying continued as revenue came in. By 1895, the trolley had 8.5 miles of track.

In 1894, Congress adopted a joint resolution specifically to try and use the power of government to stop the private company. The resolution noted that was "imminent danger that portions of said battlefield may be irreparably defaced by the construction of a railway over same" and it gave the Secretary of War the ability to acquire the land by purchase or condemnation.

The Gettysburg Railway Company refused to sell and the government began condemnation proceedings in June 1894. The trolley filed suit against the government to stop the eminent domain action. The United States Circuit Court sided with the trolley company. Judge George Dallas noted in his decision that the "powers of congress are distinctly enumerated in the constitution, and in that enumeration none is included to which the uses for which it is proposed to condemn this land can be related, without, in my opinion, enlarging the constitutional grant by grafting upon its express terms a construction so lax and comprehensive as to be subversive of its limited character."

On November 3, 1894, the jury identified $30,000 "as the measure of damage that would be done the Trolley by the proposed change". Both the government and trolley company appealed the ruling because the amount with either too low (trolley company) or too high (federal government).

"When the court eventually handed down an award of $30,000, attorneys for the company rejected the finding and filed exceptions, claiming that establishment of Gettysburg National Park was not a public purpose within the meaning of earlier legislation and that 'preserving lines of battle' and properly marking with tablets the positions occupied" were not public uses which permitted the condemnation of private property by the United States. The case finally went before the highest court in the Nation," Lee wrote.

The trolley company finally agreed on Nov. 12 to move its route from near Devil's Den if the government paid its expenses. The government refused. What's more, the federal government started condemnation on another tract of land in January 1895, which was also denied in circuit court.

Gettysburg trolley running through town. Courtesy of the Adams County Historical Society.

The case was taken to the U.S. Supreme Court, which unanimously ruled in 1896 in favor of the federal government. Justice Rufus Peckham wrote in the decision, "Can it be that the government is without power to preserve the land and properly mark out the various sites upon which this struggle took place? Can it not erect the monuments provided for by these acts of Congress, or even take possession of the field of battle in the name and for the benefit of all the citizens of the country for the present and for the future? Such a use seems necessarily not only a public use, but one so closely connected with the welfare of the republic itself as to be within the powers granted Congress by the Constitution for the purpose of protecting and preserving the whole country. It would be a great object lesson to all who looked upon the land thus cared for, and it would show a proper recognition of the great things that were done there on those momentous days. By this use, the government manifests for the benefit of all its citizens the value put upon the services and exertions of the citizen soldiers of that period."

The decision reversed the lower court rulings in favor of the Gettysburg Electric Railway and allowed the federal government to force the trolley company to relocate its route.

Lee wrote that the decision "established the principle that battlefield preservation was a public use for which the US government's Constitutional power of eminent domain could be used."

The trolley continued to operate in Gettysburg until November 1916 along a different route.

However, the United States v. Gettysburg Electric Railway Company case was part of case law and has had modern impact. It is often cited as justification for the actions taken in the Kelo v. City of New London where the city took private property from one person to give to another private entity.

11

THE MAIL MUST GO THROUGH

On February 1, 1900, a cold Thursday morning, Charles Pfeffer bundled up in a warm coat and hat, climbed aboard his wagon and started down the Baltimore Turnpike and into a footnote in Adams County History.

The United States Post Office started experimenting with Rural Free Delivery in 1891 in neighboring Carroll County. However, Harney, Md., which is located on the edge of Carroll County hadn't been included in those first RFD routes, according to Robert L. Bloom in *A History of Adams County, Pennsylvania 1700-1990*.

With the success of the program in Carroll County, other states and counties began adding RFD routes. Pennsylvania got its first two RFD routes near the end of November 1896. However, Harney area residents, who were in the county where RFD originated, still had to travel into Gettysburg or Taneytown for their mail.

Bloom writes that the residents asked George F. Young, the Gettysburg postmaster, for help. Young and a Henry Mathews, US special agent of RFD, toured the area in a buggy and laid out a plan. Pfeffer was hired at the mail carrier for the route, which was to begin in January 1900.

Not everyone was happy to get mail delivered to their homes, though. Many residents thought that the additional service would wind up increasing their taxes or postal rates and they protested the addition of the RFD route.

Shippensburg had started its first RFD route in 1899 and amid the controversy in Gettysburg, the *Star and Sentinel* reported that RFD had proven beneficial to everyone along the Shippensburg route. The newspaper reported, "it was urged in favor of it that it would be a means of education and enlightenment to those living in remote districts and this has been verified. People who never before took a newspaper are subscribing for a daily or weekly newspaper, more correspondence is exchanged and the people are coming more in touch with a world outside of their own."

How early Rural Free Delivery looked in Pennsylvania and probably Gettysburg in 1900. Courtesy of Schwenkfelder Library and Heritage Center, Pennsburg, Pa.

While public outcry couldn't delay RFD coming to Gettysburg, the postal service's slowness in delivering needed materials did. The start date had to be pushed back until the postal service could get the eight delivery boxes that were needed to Gettysburg and then have them installed along the route.

The collection boxes were needed so that people who didn't live directly on the RFD would still have a nearby location to drop off and pick up mail rather than having to make a long trip into town. People who lived along the route had to set up their own boxes on the route. The mail boxes had to be purchased from the postal service and cost anywhere from 75 cents to $3 (about $31 to $126 today). RFD was not required. If someone didn't put up a box, they would be expected to still continue traveling into Gettysburg for their mail.

"In serving the rout e, the carrier will use a horse and buggy which he must furnish at his own expense. He will carry a larger leather mail pouch similar to those used by carriers in the cities," the *Star and Sentinel* reported.

Some of the new regulations that the RFD mail carriers had to get used to were, according to Carl V. Besore and Robert L. Ringer in *A Reflection of the History of Waynesboro, Pennsylvania and Vicinity:*

- The mail carriers had to keep a count of all mail picked up on the route each day.
- Any mail the carrier collected that could be delivered before returning to the post office first had to have the carrier cancel the postage with an indelible pencil.
- The carrier had to keep postage stamps, cards, stamped envelopes and money order blanks with him. "If patrons entrusted him, the carrier could act as their agent, enclosing their money in the stamped addressed envelope given him by the patron," Besore and Ringer wrote.
- If carriers met one of the people on their route while they were driving, they could deliver their mail to them if requested but only if it cost them no time on their route.
- Carriers had to deliver registered mail and pension to the addressee's home as long as their mailbox was less than a mile off the route. If the house was further away, a note would be left in the mailbox explaining who could get the mail and where it could be obtained.
- Special delivery letters would be delivered to the addressee's house if it was within a mile of the mailbox. If the house was further away, the letter would be left in the mailbox as ordinary mail.

So on Feb. 1, Pfeffer headed down the Baltimore Turnpike around 10 a.m., picking up and dropping off mail. His first stop was a box in Two Taverns and then one in Yost's Store just south of Two Taverns and a third stop was at Strickhouser's Store on the Baltimore Turnpike. He then went south to Harney where he picked up mail from a collection box. Heading back towards Gettysburg, he stopped at a box at Barlow and one on Sedgwick and arrived back in Gettysburg about 5:30 p.m.

The 20-mile route had 800 people along it. After pickup up and dropping off 69 pieces of mail, the first day, Pfeffer quickly began average 220 pieces a day, according to the Feb. 20, 1900 *Star and Sentinel.*

Deemed a success, other routes were soon added. By April 1903, nearly 40 routes were in service or planned to be started in Adams County. Each route had at least 100 people on it. According to the Compiler, there were 12 routes from Gettysburg, 5 from Littlestown, 4 from Fairfield, 5 from York Springs, 4 from East Berlin, 3 from New Oxford, 1 from Biglerville, 2 from Ortanna, Idaville and Aspers, 1 from Tillie, Abbottstown and Bittinger.

The mail carriers were paid based on the length of their route. Routes under 16 miles paid $400 a year, routes between 16 and 20 miles paid $500 a year and routes over 20 miles long paid $600 a year.

Young, who had been vilified in 1900, said in 1903, "The ones who used me the hardest are today some of the strongest supporters of R.F.D."

12

DRAG RACING THROUGH GETTYSBURG BEFORE THERE WERE CARS

The horses resembled harnessed dragons. With each breath exhaled through their nostrils, the horses' breaths turned to vapor resembling smoke from fire-breathing dragons. They pawed at the snow on the street, waiting anxiously.

A sleigh with a driver sat behind each horse. The young men in the sleighs grinned at each other and at an unspoken signal, they snapped their whips and the horses leapt forward pulling their respective sleighs behind them.

While the sleighs might be typical vehicles of the day, if one of the drivers was Frank Deatrick, then he would be riding in in a streamlined speedster that would draw as many appreciative glances as a Ferrari would today on the roads of Gettysburg. Deatrick's sleigh, though costly, was fast and designed for racing.

"Suddenly there was the thud of rapidly galloping horses hoofs, and homes emptied along York and Chambersburg streets. Mothers dashed swiftly to make sure their children were off the street. A passing wagon drew hurriedly to the side of the road. Heads peered from doors and windows to watch the sight – Gettysburg was having another horse race," the *Gettysburg Times* reported in a 1952 article interviewing "old timers" about their childhood memories 50 years earlier.

These certainly weren't sanctioned horse races, seeing as how the streets of Gettysburg are not a race track. Boys will be boys, however, and they like to race whether it's in cars, on foot or in sleighs.

George "Pop" Hughes recalled that the races were run from the intersection of York and Hanover streets to the intersection of Springs and Buford avenues. He'd been too young to participate in any of the races at the time, but he had enjoyed watching them and wishing that he could be riding in one of the buggies or sleighs.

The races didn't last long, probably because the drivers didn't want to be around when the police arrived. They were also typically run in the morning. This was an inconvenience for residents along the impromptu racetrack, but the streets were less crowded at that hour.

A painting showing sleigh racing similar to what occurred in Gettysburg in the 19th and early 20th centuries.

The races could happen any time of the year. If there wasn't snow on the ground, then the drivers would race their buggies or simply sit astride their horses and urge them to go faster like a race jockey.

The next great love of young men—the car—was in existence at this time, but they were expensive, undependable and few and far between. However, 1902 was also the year before the Ford Motor Company opened and the famous Model T would start rolling off the assembly line in 1908. The Model T got travel as fast as a horse pulling a buggy and the view was much better for the driver.

Because young men have a need for speed and also tend to embrace technology, automobiles soon caught on in Adams County and before long, car races through towns replaced horse races. East Berlin had its first automobile race in 1910, according to the East Berlin Historical Preservation Society.

13

GETTYSBURG GOES TO THE WORLD'S FAIR

In 1904, the entire town of Gettysburg went to the St. Louis World's Fair. Not the actual town and its residents but a detailed relief map that depicted more than 24 square miles of the town and battlefield.

Engineers with the Gettysburg National Park Commission and under the direction of Emmor Cope created the maps so that "all contours were run by bearings and distances at vertical intervals of 12 feet, all topography obtained by actual surveys by the engineers and no data taken from any other source," according to the *Gettysburg Compiler.*

Cope was a veteran of the Battle of Gettysburg whose topographic map was used by the commission for its early work to survey land, build roads and build observation towers.

Secretary of War Elihu Root authorized the project and it included all the area's buildings, roads and avenues. The final scale of the map was 1:200 horizontally and 1:72 vertically and showed 24.15 square miles. The actually dimensions were 9' 3" by 12' 8".

"It is composed of successive layers of white pine strips 1/8 inch thick, out to the shapes of the corresponding contours on the topographical map, glued and pegged together," the *Compiler* reported. Each layer of wood represented 12 feet of height and each layer of wood was applied so that the wood grain ran perpendicular to the layers it was between. The sharp edges were then shaved to smooth out the contours.

The entire project took more than a year to create with the actual construction of the map taking about nine months.

"The map shows practically everything on the surface of the ground, all streams, runs, ditches and the like the division of land into fields appears, the kind of fence, whether post or rail, tapeworm, or stone, is made plain on the map; so much of the ground is covered brush, or timber is made plain. The farm buildings are all accurately located. Gettysburg on the map is a perfect miniature. The shape of the houses is preserved. Any building can be instantly recognized," the *Compiler* reported.

In 1904, this wooden relief map of the Gettysburg battlefield was first displayed at the St. Louis World's Fair. Courtesy of *GettysburgDaily.com*.

Before heading off for display in St. Louis, the relief map was placed on exhibition at the Winter Building in town on April 5 and 6 so that anyone who wanted to see the map would be able to do so.

The 1904 World's Fair ran from April 30, 1904, to December 1, 1904. It had been planned as a celebration of the 1803 Louisiana Purchase, but the opening was delayed to allow greater international participation (62 foreign counties eventually participated). The fair covered 1,200 acres in St. Louis and had more than 1,500 buildings connected by 75 miles of roads and walkways. During its run, 19.7 million people visited the fair.

While at the World's Fair, the relief was on display at the Battle Abbey building that opened on June 1. Admission was 25 cents for adults and 15 cents for children. Once in the building, they could view the map and other things like:

A recreated medieval castle (400' x 250') complete with towers, bastions, parapet and drawbridge.

A battle history and war museum of the American Republic with guides dressed historic American military uniforms.

Six plastic cycloramas that showed the battles of Yorktown (Revolutionary War, 1781), New Orleans (War of 1812), Buena Vista (Mexican War, 1846), Manassas and Gettysburg (Civil War, 1861/1863), Custer's Massacre (last stand, 1876), Manila (Spanish-American War, 1898).

After the fair closed, another wooden map was created so that one copy could be kept in Washington, D.C. and the other copy kept in Gettysburg. According to *GettysburgDaily.com*, the Gettysburg copy was kept in the county office building (the current Adams County Public Library). It was then moved to the old cyclorama building and it is now on display in the Gettysburg National Military Park Visitor's Center.

14

MASSIVE MANHUNT TO CAPTURE A CHICKEN THIEF

In 1908, a crime wave hit Adams County. Residents would rush to their windows at every sound. They would peer into the dark searching for lurking figures in the darkness. It didn't stop until a shootout and a massive manhunt ended with the capture of Ambrose Dittenhafer.

With his crime spree ended, chickens in Adams County were once again safe.

Yes, chickens.

Dittenhafer was a chicken thief.

The 53-year-old Dittenhafer had had run-ins with the law for years. Some involved animal cruelty. One was assault on a police office, but it was nighttime wholesale chicken business that sent him to jail for a significant amount of time.

However, in the late fall of 1908, chickens started disappearing from hen houses around the county. No one knew who the thief was, but they had their suspicions.

On election night, Straban Township resident Martin Harman had to go to Hunterstown for some reason. His wife followed him later in the evening. As she headed to Hunterstown, she saw Dittenhafer walking along the road. Something about the situation and Dittenhafer made her suspicious and she told her husband what she had seen when the met up with him.

Harman borrowed a gun, made sure it was loaded and headed back to his farm. He passed Dittenhafer on the way back. Harman turned off the road early to mislead Dittenhafer. Then Harman tied up his horse and hurried across a field to his property. Once there, he hid in his barn to wait.

A few minutes later, someone whose identity was hidden in shadows entered the barn.

"The dark figured selected some fat pullets roosting on the barn year fence and hurriedly placed them in a bag which he was carrying. Next he made for a willow tree near the Harman farm watering trough. Some well fattened Spring chickens were found slumbering here and Ambrose was in the act of selecting the choicest of those when Mr. Harman commenced action," the *New Oxford Item* reported.

Harman fired at the thief twice. The shots, which were probably rock salt, hit the thief. Unfortunately, Harman learned later that his shots also killed several of the chickens in the bag.

Dittenhafer shouted, "Don't shoot again!"

As Harman approached him, Dittenhafer dropped his bag and ran off. "It is said that in his efforts to escape Dittenhafer divested him of all his clothing possible and cast aside all unnecessary possessions," the *New Oxford Item* reported.

For some reason, Harman remained at large for more than a week. Then he entered the Lower Brother's Store in Table Rock on Nov. 20 and was recognized. Justice of the Peace H. B. Mears issued a warrant that Constable John F. Wolf of Butler Township served on him at the store.

"With a vigorous denial he made a dash for the door, Constable Wolf hanging on to his coat and urging the men about to help him hold the man who was fast making his exit," the *Adams County News* reported.

Dittenhafer grabbed the club he always carried and fled out the door. He ran across a nearby field "making decidedly uncomplimentary remarks about Constable Wolf on the way," the *Adams County News* reported.

Three days later, a report came in that Dittenhafer was going to return to his home.

Detective Charles Wilson, County Deputy Fred Kappes and Constable Morrison of Straban Township surrounded Dittenhafer's house and remained in hiding through the night when they thought they saw him sneak into the house.

"Detective Wilson at once rushed in and was confronted by the man's wife who had a shot gun leveled at him. Not dismayed he hurried through the various rooms after the man, being met in one of them by one of Dittenhafer's sons armed with a gun. No harm was done," the *Adams County News* reported.

However, Dittenhafer wasn't found. He had managed to escape into the foggy night.

The law officers then organized a large posse of citizens and set off on Dittenhafer's trail. They followed him for three miles through the fog only rarely catching sight of him. When he was seen, the posse would fire shots at him, apparently without hitting Dittenhafer.

He managed to double back and he returned to his house. After six hours of pursuit, the posse managed to surround him.

"Here the man realizing that his chances for escape were rather slim made a desperate fight and armed with a razor and his "big stick" was ready for a hand to hand combat. Shot after shot fired into his hiding place and he finally emerged to be met by Detective Wilson whose pistol was pointing straight at his head. Realizing that all was up he surrendered," the *Adams County News* reported.

Dittenhafer begged to be let go. He said that he would leave the county if Wilson let him go. Wilson's answer was to handcuff him and transport him to the county jail.

On February 1, 1909, Dittenhafer pled guilty of "larceny of chickens." Dittenhafer said that he would leave the county if the judge wouldn't sentence him to jail time. Instead, Judge Swope sentenced him to one year in Eastern State Penitentiary. Rebecca Dittenhafer pleaded that her husband be allowed to serve out his time in the county jail.

Swope was unmoved. He told her, "If you were to stay here she might feel that she ought to bring some food to you at the county prison and thus spend some of her energy which will be necessary for the support of the family while you are serving her sentence," the *Gettysburg Times* reported.

Dittenhafer behaved well in the penitentiary and was released a couple months early. Things did not improve for Dittenhafer as a free man.

"Nobody will give me any work and I do not have sufficient money to support my family," Dittenhafer told the *Adams County News*. "It is right in the middle of the Winter and I cannot raise any produce with which to earn a living. No one will give me a job or lend me money, and there you are. If I steal, down the road I go. I want to lead an honest and honorable life now but it's pretty hard times."

During his time in prison, his wife and children had been living in the county poor house. Dittenhafer had gotten a new suit and $10 on his release from prison. The money disappeared quickly, though. He had $3 stolen from him after he paid for car fare home from prison, and with the remainder, he bought his son, George, a new set of clothes.

By March, it was reported that Dittenhafer had finally not only left the county, but the state. He was said to be managing a farm in Maryland.

15

MAN AVOIDS GETTING SAWED IN HALF

The large, circular saw blades spun fast enough that jagged metal teeth could tear into the hard wood, cutting the thick log into two pieces. The two pieces would be further trimmed and shaped into boards and planks.

The cutting process at the Amos R. Spangler saw mill in Tyrone Township was centered around the conveyor belts. At one end of the belt, men placed logs on the belt, which carried the logs up to the spinning blades. At the blades, men would center the logs to be cut and pull off the cut pieces to be stacked. They would later be carried back to the beginning of the belt to start the journey again for trim work.

Luther Spangler was only 19 years old in in November 1908. He worked for his father at the mill as hard as any of the other workers. However, on November 27, he wasn't feeling so good. He chose not to slack off with his work, though. After all, he had a wife to support. If he didn't work, he didn't get paid.

While working loading logs onto the conveyor belt, he suddenly became light-headed and fainted. He fell onto the belt, which was about eight inches wide.

"It held him, however, and carried him at full speed so that none of those standing about could lift the unconscious form of their fellow employee from his perilous position, before he was carried up to the tightening pulley," the *Gettysburg Times* reported.

The men at the mill shouted, hoping to revive him if they couldn't reach him. Midway between the engine and the circular saw two conveyor belts met, Luther's head went under the belt and was caught between the belt and pulley.

"All of the hands who saw the accident thought that his neck was broken," the *Gettysburg Times* reported.

The men finally reached Spangler. Most of them thought that he was dead, but someone thought to check to see if his heart was still beating and they realized that Spangler was still alive.

The Kalbach and Livengood Sawmill on the Winfield Horner Farm in Zora is one of the many mills Adams County had in the early 20th Century. Courtesy of the Adams County Historical Society.

They carefully freed him from the belt and pulley and took him to his home and to his wife Emma.

Dr. Smith of Center Mills was called and he came out to the Spangler home. The doctor treated Spangler's injuries and found, "The right side of his face was badly burned and he had a number of ugly cuts about his face, head and eyes. He remained unconscious only a short while after the accident occurred and will recover in short time," according to the *Gettysburg Times.*

Luther Spangler went on to lead a long life. He and Emma had a daughter, their only child, two years later. Spangler died in 1985, having lived all his life in Adams County.

16

USING A PHONE TO FIGHT A LITTLESTOWN FIRE

Roaring fires helped keep Isaac Cromer's house and outbuildings warm during the cold January days in 1909. On January 25th, Isaac and his wife, Catherine, got called away to Gettysburg to care for Cromer's mother-in-law. That left 20-year-old John Cromer alone on the farm that was located in Adams County between Littlestown and Silver Run, Md.

While John Cromer was doing some work on the farm, stray sparks spewed from the chimney of an outbuilding and caught the newly remodeled farmhouse on fire. The house had originally been a log cabin, but when it was remodeled, clapboard had been placed on the exterior. Also, a large porch had been added to the front of the house and an addition built onto the rear.

When Cromer saw the fire, he began rushing around to try and extinguish the flames. He was working by himself, though, and was soon losing ground as the fire spread.

"Realizing that the house was doomed if he could not secure help, he ran to the telephone called the central at Littlestown and telling her what was wrong asked that she notify all his neighbors having telephones that assistance was wanted at once. Many of the farmers in that vicinity are on a rural telephone line and Littlestown exchange called all and soon had a small army of fire-fighters on the scene," the *Gettysburg Times* reported.

Rural phones at the time used a hand crank to produce enough power to ring the bells of all the telephones on the line and alert the central operator. This multiple ringing of phones, though annoying if the call wasn't for you, could allow for quick notification of multiple people at once, which was just what Cromer needed.

The group of neighbors that turned out to fight the fire didn't make any better headway in saving the house, either. The flames were spreading too quickly. Once they realized this, they concentrated instead on saving the contents of the house.

They rushed into the house and carried out furnishings, clothing and personal effects out of the house. Because of their efforts, the newspaper reported that little, if anything, that was movable was lost in the house.

"The fact that his loss was not made greater by fire loss of the contents of the building and the probably destruction of other buildings was due to the quick work of the son and the Littlestown exchange in summoning aid which proved most effective and valuable," the *Gettysburg Times* reported.

The house loss amounted to several thousand dollars, which is equivalent to about $175,000 in today's dollars.

It could have been much greater, though, had it not been for Cromer and the Littlestown central operator realizing the power of the telephone.

The country had more than three million telephones at this time that were connected with central switchboards like the Littlestown exchange. However, the majority of these phones were located in big cities. Rural areas had to make due with having multiple homes in a farming community all using the same phone line. Some farming communities were even known to use their barbed-wire fencing as telephone line to transmit signals.

17

A SILENT SHOT HITS ITS MARK?

George Wolf was not a young man anymore. At 64, he had lived a lot longer than many people. Wolf was still active, though. He worked for the Gettysburg National Park Commission hauling stone from the government quarry at Powers' Hill.

He dropped a load of stone off near Spangler's Spring on Friday, Nov. 26, 1909. That done, he called it a day and headed toward his home at the intersection of W. Confederate Avenue and Emmitsburg Road.

He was driving his cart across the small run that flowed from the Lightner Ice House pond into Rock Creek when he noticed that his horse wanted a drink. He stopped the cart and allowed the horse to lower its head and drink its fill.

He stood up on the cart to stretch out the kinks in his aging back.

"Suddenly he felt a stinging pain in his back and sank to the floor of the cart with a cry of agony. The pain was more than he could endure and, not knowing what happened, he called for help," the *Adams County News* reported.

E. M. Lightner lived along Baltimore Pike not far away. He heard Wolf's yells, but thought that it was hunters who were calling to each other. Then he realized that whoever was yelling was calling for help. He left his house and tracked down the source of the yells.

When Wolf saw Lightner, he urged him to hurry to him. "Someone struck me in the back. See how badly I am hurt," Wolf said.

He thought that someone had thrown a rock hard enough to injure him. Lightner looked at Wolf's back and saw blood. Then he saw the hole in Wolf's coat. When he told Wolf that he had been shot, Wolf couldn't believe it. "He heard no sound of a gun and saw no one for some time before the incident occurred," the *Adams County News* reported.

Lightner left Wolf lying in the cart and drove into Gettysburg to the office of Dr. H. M. Hartman. Hartman put Wolf on his examining table and looked at the wound. Wolf had been shot in the back and the bullet had passed within an inch of his spinal cord before stopping inside his body just below the skin on the right side of Wolf's body. Hartman cut into Wolf and removed a .32-caliber bullet.

Wolf's friends went out to the site the following day to conduct their own investigation into what happened. They found that "The position which he occupied and the contour of the land at that place made it impossible for the shot to have been fired from more than one direction and from that direction the person who fired the shot must have seen Mr. Wolf," according to the newspaper.

They acknowledged that it was possible that someone may have been shooting at something else and missed, but since that person would have also seen Wolf, he would have seen him fall a moment after the shot had been fired. The person would have had to realize that he shot Wolf.

Wolf's friends also told the newspaper that they believed they knew who had shot their friend. They knew who had been hunting in the area where the shooter must have been and at the time of the shooting.

There is no further mention as to whether his shooter was caught , whether the shooting was accidental or not and who the shooter was.

Wolf recovered from his injury and lived until 1920 when he died from cardiac asthma. He is buried in Evergreen Cemetery.

18

WOMAN IN BLACK SCARES GETTYSBURG

As the chill of the winter nights settled into Gettysburg in 1909, many people shunned being outside if they could. Not only was it preferable to remain warm inside but the Woman in Black couldn't get you if you were in your house.

The Woman in Black wasn't just another of Gettysburg's multitude of ghost stories. She was a real person who quickly became a myth. Imagine going about your life, cooking, reading, washing, all in the privacy of your home. The hairs on the back of your neck begin to tingle. You look around and see nothing at first. Then outside your window a shape takes forms. It is a head. The features are indistinguishable as they are cast in even more shadows than the night provides. And then the face moves off, leaving you wondering whether you've seen a ghost or a prowler.

The Woman in Black first appeared in the summer of 1909. People talked about her, but it wasn't a story that rose to the level of being considered news. However, when she returned again in late November, people began to get worried.

"Many women and children have refused to leave their homes after dark and each new rumor made their fears more intense. Not only were the female members of various families alarmed but many men are reported to have remarked that they would not care to meet her alone in the dark," the *Gettysburg Times* reported.

The woman was described as being 5 feet 10 inches tall with broad shoulders. She wore a heavy black veil and black dress. She would walk down the street, pausing to peer into windows.

"In every house women saw her and all were afraid to say anything or to investigate. Houses were locked a little more securely but nothing else done," the newspaper reported.

When the Woman in Black was seen in the summer and in late November, she was seen only on North Washington Street. Then, at the beginning of December, she began prowling South Washington Street.

"Her conduct this time is exactly the same as at the time of the visit a few months ago. No clue whatever has been obtained showing her identity and she remains as mysterious a personage as ever," the *Gettysburg Times* reported.

As rumors grew, it became difficult to be a woman wearing black in Gettysburg. On Dec. 1, the *Gettysburg Times* reported that a woman matching the scant description of the Woman in Black had been accosted on Lincoln Avenue, but it turned out to be a "domestic" from a North End home.

Another time, two men saw the Woman in Black on Chambersburg Street and began pursuing her.

"She turned South on Washington street and soon realized that she was being followed for she zig-zagged back and forth across the street in an effort to follow the dark places," the *Gettysburg Times* reported.

The woman eluded her pursuers, but the men who pursued her swore that the Woman in Black was actually a male.

On Dec. 2, the *Gettysburg Times* reported on the front page that the Woman in Black had been identified. Though not named, the Woman in Black was the domestic who had been accosted on Lincoln Avenue. It was also noted that it "is said by those who know her to be somewhat mentally deficient."

Besides working as a domestic in a North End home, she had also performed similar duties at some of Gettysburg's hotels. In the course of her work at one of the hotels, she "is said to have become infatuated with one of the employees, in search of whom she now wanders the night."

It is not noted whether the Woman in Black ever found where the man she loved lived, but she apparently stopped peeking in windows to find out.

19

FIGHTING IN THE POOR HOUSE

Adams County took responsibility for caring for its poor in 1817 by helping them care for themselves. However, things didn't always run as smoothly as one might hope.

The Adams County Almshouse was built about a mile from Gettysburg on the old Harrisburg Road. It was more than a single building. The original complex of buildings included the poor house, infirmary and insane hospital.

The poor house was a 70 by 40 feet, two-story brick house with a basement. The insane asylum was 95 by 20 feet in another two-story brick structure. The infirmary was 60 by 32 feet and was a two-story brick building. These three buildings could help 125 of Adams County's neediest at once, according to Asylumprojects.org.

The buildings were on two pieces of property northeast of Gettysburg that totaled 156 acres. The county purchased them in 1818 to support what was called the "Poor District."

"Farms were developed as part of the Poor District in many Pennsylvania counties in the hope that work on the farm would teach paupers the value of hard work in sustaining their livelihood and they would learn a skill that would help them gain employment. It was hoped that the District would be self-sustaining by farming and raising livestock, fruits and vegetables," the *Gettysburg Times* reported.

Before a person could be admitted to the almshouse, two Justices of the Peace and one Director of the Poor examined the person to verify that he or she was needy and would comply with the rules of the Poor District. Once admitted, the person became an inmate under the supervision of stewards who were usually a husband and wife who lived on the property.

The Almshouse facilities grew over the years. A bank barn was added in 1830, a smokehouse in 1831, a wagon shed in 1836, another asylum in 1878 and a women's building in 1904, according to the *Gettysburg Times*.

ADAMS COUNTY ALMSHOUSE—INFIRMARY BUILDING.
One of the buildings that made up the Adams County Alms-house. Courtesy of *Asylumprojects.org*.

"Population tripled by 1838, requiring the addition of another large brick building. In addition to the able-bodied poor people, many inmates were sick, elderly and suffered from mental illness. In 1845, another brick building was added in response to the recommendation that the inmates needed to be separated according to their needs," the *Gettysburg Times* reported.

Additional land purchases in 1831, 1840, 1846 and 1851 increased the size of the Poor District to 375 acres. Wheat, rye, oats, corn and cattle were all raised on the farm.

With so many people living in close quarters, problems could sometimes break out.

"Rough house reigned in the neighborhood of the County Home on Friday night until Detective Wilson was summoned by a hurry call and dispersed an angry crowd of knights of the road who had gotten into quite a mixup," the *Gettysburg Times* reported on November 27, 1909.

The homeless men had applied for a place to sleep overnight out of the cold weather. They were usually assigned to the pest house, which had rooms heated by stoves to serve as a cold-weather shelter for the men.

On Friday, November 26, two homeless men applied for quarters and were assigned to the alms house. Later, eight more men showed up and were also sent to the pest house for sleeping quarters.

"The early birds claimed the worm was theirs and refused to share with the double quartet. The latter threatened an invasion and in fact started to put their threat into execution when they met with vigorous resistance from the occupants of the building. Vile oaths and a lively mix-up followed. Blood flowed freely and the ten men made night hideous generally," the *Gettysburg Times* reported.

Fearing that the trouble would spread throughout the Poor District, the steward sent for the police. Detective Wilson pressed the Hotel Gettysburg bus into service as a patrol wagon and headed out to the almshouse.

By the time he arrived, one of the pair of homeless men who had started the trouble had fled. Wilson arrested the other one and gave him overnight accommodations in the county jail.

"The eight then took possession and spent a peaceful night," the newspaper reported.

The Adams County Almshouse closed down in 1964. Over the next decade, the buildings were demolished. The cemetery still remains on Barlow's Knoll.

20

LITTLESTOWN MAN
DIES OF FRIGHT

John McCall was one of the oldest engineers working on the Northern Central Railroad in 1909. He had worked for the railroad for over 30 years and even lost a leg eight years earlier in an accident on the railroad.

So what could a man who had probably seen everything—good and bad—having to do with the railroad have seen that literally scared him to death?

The Northern Central Railroad ran from Baltimore, Md., to Sunbury, Pa. It had been completed in 1858. The railroad's claim to fame was that President Abraham Lincoln rode on the railroad to deliver his Gettysburg Address in 1863, changing trains in Hanover Junction, Pa. Then in 1865, the Northern Central Railroad carried Lincoln partway on his final journey to Springfield, Ill., where he would be buried.

On Dec. 3, McCall was working on the Frederick Branch of the railroad, east of Stony Brook, at the York Valley Lime and Stone company quarries, near Hallam, Pa. He backed Locomotive No. 4134 onto a siding at the quarry and unloaded the coal with which it was filled.

After coming off that siding, he reversed the locomotive to back onto another siding. The brakeman applied the hand brakes to stop the locomotive along the siding, but it began drifting backwards down the steep grade.

"When the brakeman realized that he was unable to hold the car he shouted a warning to McCall, who may or may not have heard it. A moment later the heavy steel car side swiped the locomotive cab, tearing the right side entirely off and throwing McCall to the track, where he was pinned between the parallel bars and driving wheels of the locomotive," the *Gettysburg Times* reported.

Men nearby rushed to his aid, but McCall was trapped. In order to free him, McCall's rescuers had to saw off his wooden leg, "which was fastened under the engine in such a way that it was impossible to move the man otherwise," according to the *Gettysburg Times*.

His injuries from the accident were considered slight. McCall has a slight gash on his forehead and a broken left thumb. The most serious of his injuries was the amputation of his left index finger. These injuries were indeed slight, considering that McCall had previously survived the loss of his right leg around the turn of the century.

The accident had occurred around 5:45 p.m. and by 6:30 p.m. that evening McCall was dead. Dr. W. F. Bacon pronounced McCall dead due to shock and not his injuries. The York County coroner, J. E. Dehoff, later agreed with Bacon's pronouncement.

John's son, Carter McCall, also lived in Littlestown. He was a member of the freight crew on his father's train. He was notified of his father's death so that he could claim the body and return it to his family in Littlestown.

"The accident is the most peculiar known on the railroad, and a similar accident could not be remembered by any of the oldest engineers on the road," the *Gettysburg Times* reported.

21

THE SECOND INVASION OF GETTYSBURG

In 1913, two armies invaded Gettysburg for a second time. They had fought the first time in 1863 and were looking forward to facing each other again. It wasn't a fight that they were looking for at their second meeting, though, it was a final peace.

At the beginning of the 20th Century, Civil War veterans were aging into their 60's and 70's at a time when the average lifespan of American was around 47 years.

Acting on an idea from Henry Shippen Huidekoper, who had been wounded during the battle of Gettysburg, Pennsylvania Governor Edwin Stuart reminded the state legislature on January 5, 1909, that the commonwealth had sent 69 infantry regiments, 10 cavalry regiments and seven artillery batteries to fight and die in the war. With the 50th Anniversary of the Battle of Gettysburg approaching, Pennsylvania should find a way to honor the remaining veterans.

The reunion commissions

Gettysburg had hosted battlefield reunions before, but they were relatively small events. For this milestone reunion, people envisioned an immense event with so many people in town and the surrounding countryside as hadn't been seen since the battle itself. Gettysburg had grown from about 2,400 residents in 1863 to 4,500 in 1913, but it was still too small of a town to house all of the veterans and visitors who were expected for the anniversary. For such a reunion, preparations would have to begin early.

The legislature created the nine-member Pennsylvania Battle of Gettysburg Commission on May 13, 1909, and gave it the task of planning the 50th anniversary. The commission met for the first time in Philadelphia at the end of November and sent out its first notice announcing its plan to put together a grand reunion at Gettysburg the following month.

State legislatures responded positively and representatives were appointed from every state. They would serve as liaisons between their states and the Pennsylvania Battle of Gettysburg Commission.

Seeing the nationwide interest in the event, the U.S. Congress appointed a committee of three U.S. senators and three congressmen to assist the Pennsylvania Commission in June 1910.

Much of the federal assistance came in the form of U.S. Army personnel to plan how to run the camp and army equipment.

Tents laid out for the Great Camp at Gettysburg. Courtesy of the Library of Congress.

Planning and construction

In January and February 1912 the Pennsylvania Battle of Gettysburg Commission met with the federal commission and the War Department to begin laying out the specifics. In essence, the two commissions were building a temporary city on the battlefield that became known as the Great Camp.

It covered 280 acres and much of the battlefield south of Gettysburg. Initial plans were that the camp would contain 5,000 10-to-12-

man tents with each tent housing eight veterans. The main tent was called "The Great Tent" and was large enough to hold between 10,000 and 15,000 people. Meals would be served at kitchens at the end of each company street. Only hand baggage would be allowed in the camp. It would open on Sunday, June 29 and remain open to July 6 in order to try and avoid a crush on roads or train station.

Gettysburg had two single-track railroads, the Reading and the Western Maryland. The Army's Quartermaster Office estimated their maximum capacity would be no more than 13,000 people per day. The management of both railroad companies cooperated to make improvements and to maximize their efficiency in transporting people into and out Gettysburg for the reunion.

At the camp, water would be supplied by artesian wells that were drilled in February 1913. The water was pumped to storage containers and distributed throughout the camp via gravity. The water was cooled as it passed through coils packed in ice to deliver cold water at drinking fountains throughout the camp. Ninety latrines that could seat 3,476 people were dug as well as 95 kitchen cesspools.

It took two months to erect and equip the Great Camp.

It quickly became apparent was that the number of Civil War veterans expected to attend continued to rise past the initial estimate of 40,000. The Pennsylvania Legislature passed an emergency bill on June 23, 1913, allocating $46,000 to the reunion to care for all of the veterans in excess of 40,000. When all was said and done, the commonwealth contributed $450,000 to the reunion. Other states also provided money and in-kind contributions to help their veterans attend the reunion. In all, thirty-three states contributed funds or goods to the reunion for an estimated total of $1,033,000.

Arrival

As the veterans began arriving in Gettysburg, a controversy erupted over whether Confederate flags would be allowed. Offended Confederate veterans started talking about boycotting the reunion. The Pennsylvania Reunion Commission acted quickly to set the record straight that all flags would be allowed, though the U.S. flag would be the dominant one. This clarification satisfied most of the Confederate veterans and many of them decided to leave their Confederate flags home out of respect for the U.S. flag.

Confederate General E. J. Hunter said, "This is a united country, and has only one flag. The fact that the one flag is the flag carried by our war enemies 50 years ago means nothing any more. We left our sacred standards at home."

Veterans arriving at the Great Camp at Gettysburg for the 50th reunion of the Battle of Gettysburg. Courtesy of the Library of Congress.

William Page and William F. Brawner, two Confederate veterans of the fighting on Culp's Hill in 1863, were the first two veterans who arrive for the Grand Reunion. They reached Gettysburg around 11 a.m. on June 26 wearing their faded and worn uniforms.

"Both men were besieged immediately upon their arrival by a large party of 'boys in blue' and given the warmest sort of welcome. All during the day as they wended their way about town, the foes of fifty years ago stopped them to extend a cordial handshake and wish them the best of times during their stay here. The greeting could not have been more sincere and the men are happy as youngsters over their good time," the *Gettysburg Times* reported.

Six thousand veterans were estimated to arrive on the first day that the camp was open. Instead, 21,000 veterans arrived on June 29.

Leopold Wolf, a 78-year-old veteran from Harrisburg, had few friends and no family, but he had his memories of the war and was determined to attend the reunion. He also had his pride. He wouldn't ask for a ride to the reunion and he didn't have the $1.50 fare he would have needed to pay to get to Gettysburg.

"I thought it over and decided that I would have to walk. I bought a map of the state and with the few pennies I had and started in early Saturday morning. It did not go so bad the first day, although the sun was terribly hot. The people all along the way were just as kindly as they could be to me, and that helped me a lot. I had good places to sleep, too," Wolf said.

He started out on his 47-mile journey strong and energetic, but he was an old man and after sleeping in a barn the first night, he began to feel the miles in his aged body.

"I never went through worse agony in my life. About noon I could hardly hobble 20 feet without stopping for a rest, and when I finally struck the town I thought I would never get through it to the camp. When I did get in I just sank down on the first unoccupied cot I could find and went to sleep," Wolf said.

Temperatures in Gettysburg were in the eighties even at daybreak. Humidity remained high throughout the day. Before the camp had even officially opened, the doctors in the camp treated several cases of heat exhaustion.

With more than 50,000 senior citizens expected to stay on the battlefield, some health officials worried that there might be nearly as many casualties during the 50th reunion as there had been during the 1863 battle.

First aid services for the veterans were set up so that one of the two camp ambulances would be dispatched within minutes to pick up ill veterans. The New York Times noted that the camp was well prepared "even with facilities to perform an appendicitis operation half an hour after diagnosis." During the 50th Reunion of the Battle of Gettysburg, only nine veterans died.

Though the veterans were senior citizens, they didn't act like it. One veteran was walking through Gettysburg and asked for directions back to the camp. He was told not to attempt it because of the heat.

The veteran just shrugged and asked, "Why not? I walked all the way around Big Round Top and the Confederate line since breakfast and I guess I can go it camp without getting any more tired. I watched for the shady places and I am feeling fine."

One of the special guests to arrive was General Daniel Sickles, the last surviving Union Corps commander from the battle. The 93-year-old veteran arrived late Sunday afternoon. Escorted by a troop of U.S. Regulars, Sickles went to the Rogers House where he sat on the porch and looked out over where he had fallen after a cannonball shattered his leg. The people caring for the general estimated that he must have shaken 3,000 hands while meeting his admirers at the Rogers' House.30

"The wheat field looks the same today as it did 50 years ago. This occasion brings me to the height of my glory, and if the loss of my leg helped toward the cause of the nation, I am heartily glad. This is the best day of my life since that battle," Sickles said. "There have been times when I felt like it, but today I am a boy again., as young as you, young man, and this occasion will make me live to be 100."

Helen D. Longstreet, widow of General James Longstreet, also attended the reunion. She was given two tents to use in the camp during the reunion. This was a special honor since the camp had been reserved for veterans and staff only.

Because of the heavy volume of traffic on the rail lines, the trains approached the region slowly in order to avoid any accidents. This caused many of the trains to arrive much later than originally planned.

From midnight Sunday until noon Monday, 53 trains arrived in camp, each carrying between 200 and 500 veterans. Many of these trains were direct specials and some even had cots on which the veterans could sleep during the journey and doctors who looked after them along the way.

Veterans eventually made their way to the camp from the railroad stations only to find that there was no place for them to sleep. Some found space in the tents of their friends. Others slept outside during the warm night.

The next morning an emergency shipment of 25,000 additional blankets was ordered. Additional cots were also ordered and added to the existing tents so that they slept 10 veterans instead of eight.

With such a large turnout, the kitchens weren't equipped to feed everyone. They spread the available food around and more was ordered. Few of the veterans complained about the lack of provisions. They had all gotten by on less before, and for some of them, that time of skimpy rations had been 50 years earlier at Gettysburg.

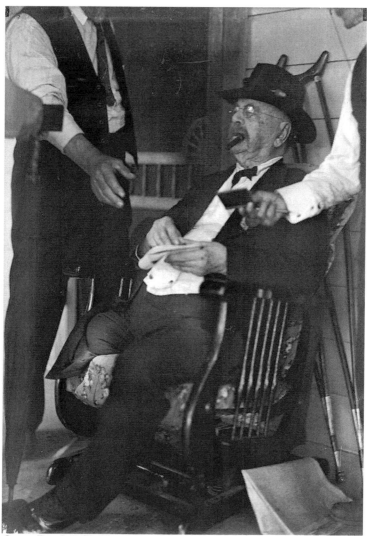

Gen. Daniel Sickles, the last surviving corps commander from the Battle of Gettysburg, returns to where he lost his leg. Courtesy of the Library of Congress.

"Two meals a day is good enough," said one veteran tonight, "that's more than we got 50 years ago."

One might think that old men arriving in Gettysburg after a long journey would be exhausted and contemplative being back in a place where many of them had nearly died. Such was not the case.

"Many of the veterans came into the encampment like a lot of boys out for a picnic. Laughing and chatting as they found their tents, calling and slapping each other on the back they frolicked about until they became weary and then sat down to talk over incidents of the war," the *Gettysburg Times* reported.

The veterans ranged in age from 61 to 112 years old. Micyah Weiss, the oldest veteran, walked using two canes. His daughter drove him to the reunion from New York, but as the camp was for veterans and staff only, he went on alone from the camp gate and had no troubles getting around among his comrades.

John Lincoln Clem was the youngest veteran in attendance and he still served as a colonel in the Army. When he was 10 years old, he had run away from home and had joined the Union Army at Shiloh as a drummer boy.

Girls of '63

On the evening before the official anniversary events began, many of the veterans gathered to honor a small group of non-veterans.

On June 30, 1863, Union General John Buford had entered Gettysburg in pursuit of the Confederate army. According to the New York Times, "Gettysburg had been in a panic all day over the appearance of the Confederates, and its joy at seeing Buford's cavalrymen in their blue uniforms knew no bounds. As the cavalrymen rode through the streets they passed through lanes of Gettysburg girls in white dresses, who sang patriotic songs all the way and strewed flowers before them."

That welcome was not forgotten. When members of the 6th New York Cavalry heard about the Gettysburg reunion, they had started thinking about those young girls and wondering whether any of them were still in the area. They scoured the town looking for the girls, now older women. Six of them still lived in Gettysburg or nearby. They were all escorted to the grandstand on June 30, 1913, while the band played a march.

Major Jerome B. Wheeler of the 6th New York Cavalry said to them, "If absence makes the heart grow fonder, how our hearts go out to you to-day as we look into your dear faces after an absence of fifty years. We left you most sorrowfully and regretfully, and we now come to you from all parts of the country to tender our regret that our first visit was so brief and our years of absence so inevitable. And we to thank you and say, 'God Bless You' for the friendly greeting you extended to us in those days so long ago, when kind words from gentle and noble women were like an oasis in a desert."

The soldiers then called on the women to sing one of the songs they had sung 50 years previously.

"Whether the voices were or were not so good as they were fifty years ago, they sounded clear and sweet in the big tent, and no grand opera singer ever had such an appreciative audience. The old men listened as if they were hearing Melba. Many of them were wiping their eyes," reported the *New York Times.*

Veteran stories

As veterans continued arriving, one Virginia veteran went looking for his tent in the Great Camp. He walked from tent to tent, opening the flap and asking any veterans inside where he could find his regiment. Finally, the lost Johnny Reb wandered into the area where survivors of the 1st Minnesota Regiment, which had suffered 82 percent casualties at Gettysburg, were staying.

At the fifth tent he came to, the Minnesotan inside asked, "And who were you with, Johnnie?"

"Twenty-eighth Virginia," the former Confederate replied.

"That would be Olmstead's men?"

"Right. And we met you 1st Minnesota fellows off yonder— there where the lightning was thickest."

"Well, I'll be damned."

Showing that any past animosity was forgotten, the group welcomed their former enemy into the tents. They sat around out of the hot sun talking and reminiscing over liquor.

Veterans at the reunion toured the battlefield and reminisced. Courtesy of the Library of Congress.

One of the Minnesotans asked, "Say, do you know what became of the 28th Virginia's flag that day up yonder?"

"I don't," said the old Confederate. "You see, I was with Armistead's brigade, the one that got into the Yankee lines when Pickett made his charge and made what they call the 'high-water mark' of the rebellion." I don't rightly remember just what happened to the flag after we jumped into those Yankee batteries but I think some of you Yankees got it."

"We did," said the man in the tent. "I'm Capt. T. H. Pressnal of Company F, 1st Minnesota. We captured your flag, and we've got it now in St. Paul. The other fellows in this tent will be in in a minute, and all of them belonged to the regiment that got your flag. We've got a spare blanket here and you'll never find your tent to-night. Come in and bunk with us."

Since the night was getting darker, the Virginian accepted the offer. In the morning, he told his hosts, "You know, I've been a-lyin' here thinkin'. As long as some of you Yanks had to get that flag, I'm mighty glad it were you-all. You're right good people."

Out on the battlefield, a gray-bearded Confederate veteran of Pickett's Charge, A. C. Smith of Virginia, was telling of his experience during the charge. He walked along Cemetery Ridge with fellow Confederates.

"Well, here I was. And right here's where I leaped across. I got a yard beyond that wall, I reckon, when I got hit and down I went. I remember a chap in blue runnin' at me. He had a bayonet, and I thought I was a goner. But he give me a drink of water from his canteen. And then blamed if he didn't pick me up and carry me off to a Yank hospital.

"I never saw him again. I reckon he's gone to his reward by this time," Smith told the veterans in his group.

Another group of veterans was nearby listening to a Union veteran recount his story. R. N. Hamilton said, "The Rebs got to about here. Then we beat 'em back. And it was right here..." Hamilton pointed to the wall. "...that a Johnny fell into my arms. I lifted him up and gave him a swig from my canteen. Then I got him on my shoulders and carried him off."

Smith heard Hamilton and drew closer to get a good look at the man. He shouted, "Well, Praise the Lord; Praise the Lord it's you, brother."

The two men embraced and Hamilton said, "Fifty years ago. Don't that beat all!"

Other reunions didn't end so happily. One former Union soldier in his faded blue uniform found the person he was looking for in the Soldiers' National Cemetery beneath a small tombstone that read "William Henry Scott."

He held his cap in his hand as tears rolled down his cheeks.

"After the first day's fighting, they carried me into a hospital, badly wounded," the soldier said to his companions. "Next to me was a young Southerner, from Georgia. We two chummed up in the hospital and he told me his name was William Henry Scott. He told me of his plantation and I told him of my home in New York. We came to love each other, promised when each got better that we'd come and visit one another. I was sent home; he stayed behind to get well. But he never came to see me."

The man paused in his storytelling and shook his head. "Hoped to see him here. And here he is; here he is."

By July 2, the temperature had climbed to 102 degrees in the shade. The beastly hot weather changed in the afternoon as heavy rains fell along with strong winds, loud thunder and violent lightning. The veterans took shelter in the camp tents and shared stories as the rain settled the dust on the roads and cleaned the canvas tents. While the rains kept the veterans under canvas and off the battlefield, they did enjoy the cooler temperatures that came with the rain.

The storm lasted about an hour and afterward, the veterans then went back onto the battlefield.

The last surviving Confederates re-enact Pickett's Charge. They were met at the end of the "charge" by the last surviving Union Veterans from the charge. Courtesy of the Library of Congress.

Pickett's last charge

The July 3 events featured 11 governors, Vice President Thomas Marshall and Speaker of the House of Representatives, Champ Clark speaking before the veterans. However, the highlight of the day was a re-enactment of Pickett's Charge with the surviving veterans.

The two lines formed a quarter mile apart. The Philadelphia Brigade stood the north and Pickett's Division on the south side of the stone wall, over which they had fought so desperately fifty years earlier.

"There were no flashing sabers, no guns roaring with shell, only eyes that dimmed fast, and kindly faces behind the stone wall that marks the angle. At the end, in place of wounds or prison or death, were handshakes, speeches, and mingling cheers," the *Washington Post* reported.

From the thousands who had made the daring charge in 1863, only 150 Confederate soldiers remained to repeat the charge.

Rep. J. Hampton Moore, of Philadelphia, a congressman from the 3rd Pennsylvania District, presented on behalf of the Philadelphia Brigade Association to the Pickett's Division Association a beautiful silk flag of the United States.

That evening the veterans were treated to a fireworks display shot off from the top of Little Roundtop. The sound of the show was so loud that it frightened many veterans. A few of them were thrown back to 1863 and started shouting, "Down, boys! Lie down! Steady."

The final day of the reunion was July 4th. What better way to celebrate the peace and unity among former enemies than to have both sides join in the celebration of united country?

President Woodrow Wilson was the special speaker for the day. He was a good choice. Not only was he the current commander-in-chief of the U. S. military, but his father had owned slaves and briefly served in the Confederate Army.

The response to the Wilson's speech was mixed. He praised the veterans for their service, saying that they had set an example for the nation. He said the veterans were looking to the current generation to "perfect what they had established. Their work is handed unto us, to be done in another way but not in another spirit." He then went on to say what the nation faced then was greater than what it had faced 50 years earlier.

As veterans prepared to return home on July 5, a few of them made one last visit to the battlefield to find a memento.

Jefferson Sefton of Dubuque, Iowa, took home two suitcases of soil from the battlefield.

"This is more precious to me than anything else. I fought on the spot where I gathered this soil, and I want to take some of it back home. I shall make a garden box of it," Sefton said.

Though 54,000 is the oft-quoted figure for how many veterans attended the reunion, the New York State Commission for the reunion estimated it as 70,000 with 55,000 of them staying in the camp.

22

CAMP COMMAND BROUGHT EISENHOWER TO GETTYSBURG FOR THE FIRST TIME

More than 8,700 Confederate Army veterans lived to attend the 50th anniversary reunion of the Battle of Gettysburg in 1913. They camped on the field where General George Pickett and his men had made their brave charge more than mile across an open field into the cannons on the Union Army in July 1863.

Veterans of that charge would have been among the old men attending the reunion. They would have looked at the field covered with tents where the veterans camped during the reunion and remembered that the ground had been covered with bodies 50 years earlier. In that desperate charge, many of the unprotected soldiers had been felled by bullets.

Had the veterans returned five years later, they still would have seen tents on the field where so much Confederate blood had been shed. They would have also seen something that would have given them pause, for had Pickett's men had it in 1863 rumbling across that open field as it was in 1918, Pickett's Charge would have succeeded.

Tanks in war

Though the idea of a tank had been around since Leonardo da Vinci conceived of an armored wagon, the idea of using a tank in war didn't come about until 1903, and then, it still took until 1915 to develop a practical model. With the start of World War I and the

United States' entry into the conflict, the U.S. Army began to look for a way to integrate tanks into the service.

Capt. Dwight Eisenhower poses with one of Camp Colt's tanks. Courtesy of the National Park Service.

The Camp with no name

An unnamed U.S. Army camp was first established on the Gettysburg battlefield in May 1917. The reason it had no name, according to the 1918 Report of the National Military Park Commission, was because "we believe it is the practice when the location is at a conspicuous place on United States land, notably battle fields, such as Gettysburg." The initial location was part of the Codori farm and land where the Round Top branch of the Gettysburg and Harrisburg Railroad was located. The railroad was one of the reasons the army chose the location. It made it easy to move men and equipment directly into and out of the camp.

The camp soon grew as more and more soldiers and supplies were shipped to the camp. Each regiment had 15 or 16 wooden barracks that needed to be constructed. These were not insulated barracks or even fully completed. This temporariness of the construction showed that the camp would not be suitable as a winter quarters for men.

Even though the land where General Pickett had charged would soon be trampled by soldiers once again, the U.S. Army was not ignorant of the historical significance of the park land. In a letter to the Gettysburg Battlefield Commission, the commander of the 61st U.S. Infantry wrote, "...every effort will be made by myself to see that the enlisted men of the 61st infantry do not molest in any way, the monuments, trees, shrubbery, woods, etc. of the Gettysburg National Park.'"

Camp Colt was located south of Gettysburg on the Civil War battlefield. Courtesy of the National Park Service.

As the soldiers were shipped into the camp, three regiments of infantry were housed on the east side of Emmitsburg Road and one regiment was on the west side. An additional regiment was housed on the west side of the road along with a bakery, hospital and motor ambulance pool. Two more regiments were housed near where the Gettysburg Recreation Park is located.

Water and sewer lines were constructed to deal with the sanitary issues thousands of men would cause. The number of men at the camp grew to 8,000 at its peak, which was roughly the same population as Gettysburg at the time. The men trained through the summer, but by the end of November only a small detachment of men remained because the camp was not suitable to house soldiers through the cold Pennsylvania winters.

The new camp was named for Samuel Colt, the inventor of the Colt Peacemaker, and the camp was called Camp Colt. Equipment for tank training was moved from Camp Meade in Maryland to Gettysburg where Camp Colt occupied 176 acres of the Codori farm, 10 acres of the Smith farm and 6 acres of Bryan House place. Much of the current Colt Park housing development was also part of the camp.

The training program Eisenhower developed had soldiers practicing with machine guns mounted on flatbed trucks instead of tanks. They learned to repair engines and to use Morse Code. "At times, HQ entertained English officers who had early war experience with the first English constructed tanks on French battle fields. They came to advise on training. Then again, a few members of Congress would arrive to get a peep at the one and only tin can of a tank which was used for partial training of tankers, especially those small men, who could easily climb into its interior. A 200-pound man just couldn't," recalled George Goshaw in a 1954 *Gettysburg Times* article. He had served at the camp under Eisenhower.

Each time a call for tankers to join the fighting in Europe came, battalions of men were moved to Hoboken, New Jersey, where they boarded transports to Europe. There, they joined the fighting climbing inside of real tanks and facing real bullets and mortars.

The camp did manage to get two Renault tanks to use by the time that summer arrived. Over the nine months the camp existed more than 9,000 men were trained to fight in the war.

By October, many of the men had been transferred elsewhere because there were no suitable winter quarters. However, worse than winter weather happened in the fall of 1918. Spanish Flu swept across the world killing an estimated 50 million people, including 160 at Camp Colt, according to the Gettysburg *Star and Sentinel*. At one point during the month, the bodies literally began to pile up. The dead soldiers were taken to the Grand Army of the Republic Hall in town until arrangements could be made to ship their bodies home. As each body was taken to the depot, it was given a military escort through Gettysburg.

Capt. Dwight Eisenhower (right) poses with another officer at Camp Colt. Courtesy of the National Park Service.

Closing the camp

As the flu abated, so did the war. The armistice ending World War I was signed on November 11, 1918. "When November 11th came upon us, Ike and his entire staff were saddened, knowing full well that they were cheated out of actual battle service," Goshaw recalled. "From then on, there was a let down on training and the necessary daily duties."

The orders to close Camp Colt came on November 17. Then remaining men were sent to Camp Dix in New Jersey for their final discharge.

Veterans of the camp soon began organizing reunions in Gettysburg, although there was no longer a camp to visit. The first reunion in the 1940's was marked with the planting of the large pine tree on the east side of Emmitsburg Road south of the entrance to the old visitor's center. The tree was planted in remembrance of the tankers' fallen comrades. You can still see it today along with a commemorative plaque summarizing the history of Camp Colt.

23

THE SPANISH FLU HITS ADAMS COUNTY

In 1918, the world was at war. Though it was a different war and a different century, Gettysburg found itself once again occupied by an army. Young men were sent there to learn to fight the Germans in World War I.

They trained to fight the enemy using a piece of state-of-the-art military technology called the tank. The problem was that no one could see their enemy that they were fighting in Gettysburg. It moved indiscriminately through camps and communities injuring and killing men, women, soldier, children. It made no difference.

This war waged for about a year until the enemy retreated and hid but not before killing, by the worst estimate, about 50 million people or more than 4 times the population of Pennsylvania died.

Spanish flu

It was not World War I that killed all those people. It was the Spanish Flu. It was called Spanish Flu because it apparently first appeared in Spain, but it was simply that year's flu strain. And when it first appeared in the U.S. in the spring of 1918, it was a fairly typical flu. It was highly contagious, but it wasn't any more deadly than a typical flu strain. The problem with the flu virus is that it mutates and some of those mutations can become deadly.

Remember the SARS scare? That killed a few hundred people out of a worldwide population of 6.9 billion.

Now imagine the terror people felt about a flu that killed 50 million people when the world's population was less than 1.9 billion. Then 2-3 people out of every 100 across the world died. If the Spanish Flu struck today, the lethality would be around 180 million.

The Spanish Flu killed more people than World War I and in a shorter time frame, too, yet the war had the headlines during 1918 because it was winding down at the same time the Spanish Flu was reaching its peak. It was estimated that 675,000 Americans died from the Spanish Flu or 10 times more than died in the war.

It killed more people in one year than the Black Plague did in 4 years.

It was so devastating that human life span was reduced by 10 years in 1918.

Here's how a Spanish Flu attack was described. One physician wrote that patients rapidly "develop the most vicious type of pneumonia that has ever been seen" and later when cyanosis appeared in patients "it is simply a struggle for air until they suffocate." Another doctor said that the influenza patients "died struggling to clear their airways of a blood-tinged froth that sometimes gushed from their mouth and nose."

Here's how it was described in *Flu* by Gina Kolata:

> The sickness preyed on the young and healthy. One day you are fine, strong, and invulnerable. You might be busy at work in your office. Or maybe you are knitting a scarf for the brave troops fighting the war to end all wars. Or maybe you are a soldier reporting for basic training, your first time away from home and family.
>
> You might notice a dull headache. Your eyes might start to burn. You start to shiver and you will take to your bed, curling up in a ball. But no amount of blankets can keep you warm. You fall into a restless sleep, dreaming the distorted nightmares of delirium as your fever climbs. And when you drift out of sleep, into a sort of semi-consciousness, your muscles will ache and our head will throb and you will somehow know that, step by step, as your body feebly cries out "no," you are moving steadily toward death.

The flu can also mutate and move from humans to pigs and birds. That is why people were worried about avian flu or swine flu. They can mutate and make the jump from animal to human and be deadly.

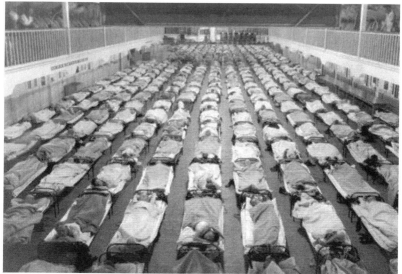

Spanish flu victims at an emergency hospital in Washington, D.C. Large buildings in Adams County were also used as emergency hospitals. Courtesy of the Library of Congress.

In Adams County

Spanish Flu first appeared in Adams County around the end of September 1918. It almost always it made its first appearance in any community during the last week of September, whether it was here or in Europe where there was fighting. This could indicate that that there wasn't a flash point location so much as this was the strain that had developed in 1918 and mutated. That is a point that is argued, though. Some have tried to set an origin point. Boston and in Kansas are the most-common locations suggested.

The *Gettysburg Compiler* reported on Sept. 28 that the flu had broken out in Camp Colt, Gettysburg's army training camp. At this point, they believed that it had come from soldiers who had been exposed to it in Camp Devens in Massachusetts, which is one of the places in an area where the flu was believed to have started.

To combat it at Camp Colt, 500 soldiers were getting daily throat sprays, which were believed enough to stop the flu. The newspaper reported, "The epidemic seems to be well in hand with treatment before the severe stages." However, within this first week of breaking out, 125 men had been hospitalized and five had died. These were the men who had come from Camp Devens.

Another factor that may have played into the spread of the flu and how deadly it was that the U.S. was sending soldiers into military camps all across the country. These camps were by and large tent camps, which I'm sure weren't conducive to staying healthy in the winter. They were also overcrowded in many cases.

Is it any wonder that the flu found fertile ground in a military camp? I think this also partially explains the W-shaped death curve of the flu. Generally, when flu is fatal, it is with the youngest and oldest in the population, those whose immune systems were weakest. Spanish Flu also spiked in the middle with 20-30 year olds roughly. This would be the age range for soldiers, particularly those who were living in tighter quarters and unhealthier conditions than they might have been ordinarily.

During the first week of the outbreak, no mention was made of the problem in the local papers. Out of sight, out of mind. Yet, the problem was growing.

It had already reached epidemic status in Pittsburgh and Philadelphia by Oct. 4. Also, by the middle of October, the state reported that there had been 6,081 deaths from the flu and 2,651 deaths from pneumonia, which was a complication of the flu. Also, the thing to remember and was widely reported all over the world is that doctors were so overwhelmed that many deaths didn't get reported.

The *Compiler* ran this headline in early October, which seemingly came out of nowhere since the paper hadn't been reporting on the buildup to it: "The Answer to the Scourge is a Demonstration by Community to Flight It to the Limit. Never has Gettysburg been so stirred as by the scourge of Influenza. Never has the heart of the town been so wrung as by the scourge carrying off the soldier boys who as answered their country's call in defense of her principles."

Father W.F. Boyle offered Xavier Hall as a hospital. Sixty-four cots were set up in the hall as it was transformed into an emergency hospital. Prof. Lamond, who was director of the Red Cross locally, sent for nurses to care for the sick and the Soldier's Club House on Middle Street was converted into the temporary living quarters for the nurses. In a show of community spirit, Mrs. Burton Alleman of Little-stown had schoolchildren canvass the town for donations for the hospital. They raised $100 and collected 59 water bottles, 10 fountain syringes, 15 ice caps, 500 sputum cups and 25 serving trays.

Father Boyle believed that it would be easier to control the flu if you could isolate the sick from the healthy. It was a good idea, but it was too late.

Two days after the hospital opened, the county schools were closed, which was a common defense against the flu. It was also announced that in less than two weeks, there were 92 dead at Camp Colt.

By Oct. 12, about three weeks after flu broke out, the *Compiler,* which had just a few days before proclaimed the flu abating, now said that it was the "most heartrending epidemic the town has ever been through. ... Distress has pervaded the hearts of our people but around this dark cloud is the glow of the wonderful demonstration of our people in town and country and nearby places."

Around this time is when people start getting worried. Body counts scare them, especially when there's little they could do about it. Warnings were issued and sick families were quarantined. Some people even took to wearing masks, just like they did when they feared SARS.

Camp Colt now had 100 dead soldiers. This was one out every six soldiers at the camp and many of the 500 remaining were sick with the flu.

The newspaper also said that Father Boyle's act helped control deaths. Not really. His goal had been to contain the sickness, but several of the nurses caring for the soldiers contracted the flu and wound up becoming patients themselves. One of the nurse aides also died from the flu. Even Professor Lamond caught the flu.

This is one of the insidious ways that the Spanish Flu worked. Many communities were already shorthanded medically because doctors had been drafted to serve in WWI. Then along came the flu, which intensified by the shortage by making many of the remaining doctors sick at a time when the workload was drastically increasing. The remaining doctors found themselves working longer hours with contagious people. This would wear them down and make them susceptible to flu and the process would repeat.

By this time, the bodies were beginning to pile up, literally. The dead soldiers were taken to the Grand Army of the Republic Hall in town until arrangements could be made to ship their bodies home. As each body was taken to the depot, it was given a military escort. This must have been a depressing sight for residents to see 100 times as each soldier was taken to the train that would return him home.

Half of the front page was being taken up with obituaries of people who died from the flu.

In one instance, George Pretz was the author of the lyrics for the Gettysburg College fight song. He was an army doctor who died in Syracuse. When his wife, Carrie, heard he was sick, she started up to New York, but she didn't arrive until after he had died. His brother-in-law, Edgar Tawney, "went to Hanover on Monday for flowers and while sitting in an automobile was stricken and being brought home died early Tuesday morning."

By mid-October, all pretense of optimism was gone. The *Gettysburg Times* had an article with the ominous headline, "Death's Harvest Still Continues."

But then a week later, the reports were suddenly upbeat. The Times declared that the flu was all but gone from Camp Colt.

As side story that began to percolate was that Health Officer F.Y. Stambaugh in Hanover was accused of negligence in caring for the sick. He was accused of failing to look after quarantine families and fumigate houses marked for flu.

A similar story to this one is that George Stravig son, brother and sister all died within a week of each other because of the flu.

Through November, there truly was a lessening of the flu cases. People started to breathe a sigh of relief. Then Adams County then suffered what only a few places around the country saw, a second spike in the flu.

Also, by the end of October, the *Times* was reporting that 23,000 Pennsylvanians had died from the flu. That represents roughly ¼ of 1 percent of the state's population that died in October and the month still had five days left in it when this was reported.

The U.S. Department of Health and Human Services estimates that the flu peaked in Philadelphia during the week of Oct. 16. On that day, not that week, that day, 700 Philadelphians died. Pittsburgh saw its peak three weeks later. So Adams County most likely saw its peaks somewhere in between.

The emergency hospital at Xavier Hall quarantine was lifted at the end of the month and by this point 148 people who had been sent there had died.

By the end of October, there was a sense of confusion about the flu. The way it was striking across the county was inconsistent. The Halloween parade in town was cancelled, but the bans about public gatherings were slowly being lifted.

Yet, the tragedies continued.

Police in many cities wore face masks to keep from getting the flu. Courtesy of the Library of Congress.

Second Time Around

The second wave hit particularly hard in the Fairfield area and the eastern part of the county. One doctor was quoted in the *Star and Sentinel* as saying, "I have just come from four homes. Three or four people were sick in every one of them. One of the families had both parents and the two children ill. I have another family in which there were six cases."

Reports said the second outbreak wasn't as pervasive, but it could still be deadly. This is typical of locations where there was a second outbreak. I have a theory about that. In the early part of 1918, the world experienced a typical flu outbreak. It wasn't deadly, but what was discovered by researchers was that people who had that flu fared much better during the Spanish Flu outbreak in the fall than those who didn't catch the spring flu. This is because the spring flu caused those people to develop antibodies that helped them fight off the Spanish Flu.

Adams County moved into the 1918 Christmas season cautiously. Dr. B. F. Royer told the *Gettysburg Times*, "With the approach of the holiday season too much stress cannot be laid on the necessity of avoiding crowding in the stores, many of which are poorly ventilated."

People were urged to do their shopping early when fewer people would be in the stores.

In another double death, the *Compiler* reported that the Stoner died within 24 hours of each other. They were farmers who had been married for two years and were both in their mid-20s.

The *Gettysburg Times* reported that Charles Walter who had been sick for 2 weeks with the flu died on January 2 at home of his parents just before they had to leave for the funeral of their daughter who had died earlier from flu.

The *Gettysburg Times* reported another unusual case associated with Spanish Flu. A man named Roy Dice said he caught the flu, survived and Dr. Swan told him he could start sitting up. He began to feel pains in his leg. It quickly swelled up and turned blue. Then gangrene set in and he would up having to have his leg amputated.

Christmas 1918 was somber. A lot of people had lost someone they knew to the flu. Church Christmas programs were cancelled for fear of having too many people in a confined space.

The *Star and Sentinel* reported on January 18 that 160 soldiers had died from the flu, most of them at Camp Colt and 19 civilians in Gettysburg and 4 in Cumberland, Straban, Freedom, Highland. This is incorrect simply from a browsing of the obituaries. Not knowing the source of their numbers, I suspect that it may be only people who listed the flu as cause of death, but pneumonia deaths were from the flu, too. Pneumonia is what the flu developed into.

Even with these numbers, Gettysburg's population was 4600 at the time. This represents roughly 4 percent of population dying.

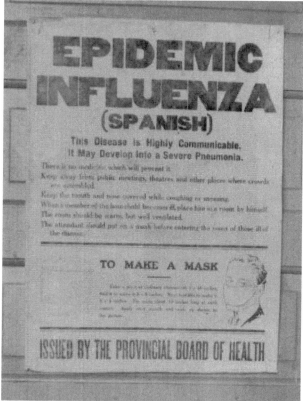

Handbills like this were posted in communities around the world to try and help stop the spreading of the flu. Courtesy of the Library of Congress.

24

EDDIE PLANK: GETTYS-BURG'S LEGENDARY LEFTY

P is for Plank,
The arm of the A's;
When he tangled with Matty
Games lasted for days.

"Lineup for Yesterday" by Ogden Nash

Though he was known as Gettysburg Eddie, his real name was Edward Stewart Plank. He was a hero to many, but not because he had fought and survived on Gettysburg's battlefield.

Gettysburg Eddie fought on a different battlefield. He held a mound of earth surrounded by a diamond-shaped field. He held it week after week, year after year, and he did it by hurling a baseball.

Gettysburg Eddie was the first left-handed pitcher in baseball history to win 200 games and then the first to win 300 games. Even today, he has the third-most wins among left-handed pitchers—326— and ranks 11th among all pitchers.

Plank was born on August 31, 1875, on his family's farm north of Gettysburg in Straban Township. Like many young boys, he took up the game of baseball as a favorite summertime activity to play with his friends. He would practice his pitching by throwing a baseball against a hay stack propped up against the wall of the barn, all the time working for greater accuracy and speed with his pitches. He brought together his brothers and friends to form the Good Intent Baseball Team and through hard work, they became the best team in Adams County, thanks in no small part to Plank's pitching.

As a young man, he attended Gettysburg Academy, a prep school for Gettysburg College. Even though he never attended or graduated from the college, he did play for the college's baseball team from 1900 to 1901, which could be considered where he began his illustrious career.

PLANK, PHILA. AMER.

One of Eddie Plank's early baseball cards.

One particular college game changed his life. Charles Albert "Chief" Bender was a popular college pitcher at Dickinson College who had an impressive win streak. Plank faced him in 1901 in a game that went 15 innings before Gettysburg College emerged the victors.

Connie Mack, owner of the Philadelphia Athletics, was in the stands watching the game at the request of Gettysburg Coach Frank Foreman. Impressed with the pitching during the game, Mack signed both pitchers. Bender was sent to the minor league team and Plank was sent to Philadelphia to play in the majors.

Early baseball

Plank grew to adulthood at the same time baseball was growing into the game we know today. Though baseball was played in the late 1700s, nine-inning games didn't become official until 1857. A pitching line of 60.5 feet didn't become standard until 1893.

Until the year Plank was born, pitchers could only throw underhanded. The first sidearm pitches, a pitch Plank favored, were allowed in 1874 and overhand pitches came about 10 years later. Pitching rubbers came into being in 1893. A pitching rubber is also called the pitcher's plate and is located on the pitcher's mound 18 inches behind dead center of the mound. The mound slopes toward home plate from the pitching rubber.

Gloves didn't become commonly used until the 1870s. Some players still played without gloves even in Plank's early years of play.

The majors

Plank made his professional baseball debut on May 13, 1901, as a Philadelphia Athletic. The team had a mediocre 10-game opening to the season. Plank made his pitching debut while the Athletics were on the road, during which time the Athletics' record began improving.

His debut in the Athletics' hometown was in June 1901 during a game against the Detroit Wolverines. The field had been resodded and 11,000 visitors filled the stadium to capacity to root for their home team.

"Young Plank made his local debut and he was immediately installed a favorite by the spectators, who lent him all sorts of encouragement as the game progressed," reported the Philadelphia Inquirer.

Eddie Plank warms up for a baseball game. Courtesy of Wiki-media Commons.

Plank held Detroit to only four hits and Philadelphia won the game 6-1.

Gettysburg Eddie played with the Athletics until 1914. During half of those years, he won more than 20 games in a season. He became known for his sidearm curve ball. He also took a long time between pitches, which some critics said extended the length of the games.

Plank's pitching helped the Athletics win the World Series in 1911 and 1913. The Athletics defeated the New York Giants in both series (4 games to 2 in 1911 and 4 games to 1 in 1913). Plank would have been in three championship games except that his arm was sore in 1910 and he had to sit out the games. Following the 1913 series win, Plank was named the series' most-valuable player for his winning performance against Christy Mathewson in the final game of the series.

The 1911 Philadelphia Athletics. Courtesy of Wikimedia Commons.

Following the win, the town of Gettysburg threw a banquet in honor of its favorite son in November. During the banquet, Judge S. McC Swope told Plank, "Eddie, we are glad you were born here. You are a credit to the town. There is not a hamlet in these Unites States however small that does not know the name of Eddie Plank and where he is from."

In 1915, Plank became a St. Louis Terrier in the Federal League. He won 21 games that season, which would be his last 20-plus win season.

The following two years Plank played for the St. Louis Browns until he retired after the 1917 season ended at the age of 41. For the winningest southpaw in the game, Plank lost his final game 1-0, pitching against Walter Johnson.

Plank's career stats were 326 wins, 194 losses, a 2.35 earned run average and 2,246 strikeouts. He pitched 69 shut-out games and 410 complete games during his career.

Retirement

Plank had saved well during his professional career so that when he retired he and his brother, Ira, were able to open up the Plank Garage in 1923 at the corner of York and Stratton streets in Gettysburg.

Though asked to pitch in many area games, Plank declined all of the offers except the chance to pitch in the annual Gettysburg College varsity versus alumni game. His decision to pitch in this game may have been influenced by that fact that Ira, a future College Hall of Fame coach, was the varsity baseball coach.

Then in 1926, 50-year-old Plank suffered a stroke that paralyzed his left side and left him unconscious for most of the time. Plank died at home on February 24, a few days after his stroke, with his wife, Anna; 10-year-old son, Eddie Plank III; and two brothers at his bedside. He is buried in Evergreen Cemetery on Baltimore Street.

The *Philadelphia Inquirer* obituary for him began this way:

> Eddie Plank is dead.
> Baseball's greatest southpaw moundsman is dead. He struck out on one pitch of mortal man's most vicious opponent, Death. A stroke of paralysis that maimed his left side and crippled his mighty left arm proved fatal early Wednesday afternoon. There was no comeback. It was not an extra inning game. It was a one-sided battle with the Grim Reaper playing the leading role against Eddie Plank, one time prem-

ier hurler of Connie Mack's million-dollar Athletics, cast in a mediocre assignment that afforded no opportunity to display his courageous ability.

Following his death, Gettysburg College honored its most-famous baseball player by naming the Eddie Plank Memorial Gymnasium during commencement week on June 7, 1927. The building contained a gymnasium, social center, armory and auditorium.

Long-lasting legacy

Plank's impressive career left a long-lasting legacy that continues years after his death.

In 1946, he was inducted into the Baseball Hall of Fame, and in 1999, The Sporting News ranked him as the 68th greatest baseball player in 1999. He was also a nominee for the Major League Baseball All-Century Team.

His Hall of Fame plaque reads: "Edward S. Plank. One of the greatest left-handed pitchers of major leagues. Never pitched for a minor league team, going from Gettysburg College to the Philadelphia A. L. Team with which he served from 1901 through 1914. One of few pitchers to win more than 300 games in big leagues. In eight of 17 seasons won 20 or more games."

25

KING TUT DANCES AT GETTYSBURG COLLEGE

In late November 1922 in faraway Egypt, Howard Carter used a chisel to make a small hole in the doorway of an ancient tomb of the boy king Tutankhamun.

"Can you see anything?" asked Lord Carnarvon, the chief financial backer of Carter's Egyptian dig.

Even by candlelight, Carter could see gold and ebony treasures inside the tomb that hadn't been raided.

"Yes, wonderful things," he told Lord Carnavon.

Also, within that tomb was the sarcophagus of Tutankhamun, which contained his mummy.

King Tut became quickly became an international celebrity who put in appearance at the Gettysburg College senior prom a few months later.

On February 9, 1923, the junior class put together a prom at the college. The academy building was transformed into Ancient Egypt. *The Gettysburgian* noted that the hall had been "Skillfully decorated with streamers of crepe paper and painted designs in orange, blue, canary, and green. An Egyptian effect was maintained through, appropriate figures coving the walls, and pretty festoons hiding the ceiling, with arches and centerpieces and lamp decorations."

The Ten Virginians band from Charleston, W.Va., provided the music for the evening.

"One could easily imagine that we were back in the days of the 'Arabian Night's Tales' and that the 'Prep' building was situated where the 'dreamy Nile doth flow'," the 1924 *Gettysburg Spectrum* reported. "One needed but to half close his eyes and dream, to imagine that he were in the palaces of the Pharaoh's."

The festivities began at 8 p.m. as couples began dancing the night away. During an intermission in the music, it was announced that King Tutankhamun would be putting in an appearance at the dance.

A dance card from the 1923 Egypt-themed junior prom. Courtesy of the Musselman Library Special Collections and Archives.

"A surprising effect was produced when three colored children, as 'slaves,' brought the little 'Egyptian' beauty into the room in a mummy case. Rising and bowing to the company, she then rendered a characteristic Egyptian dance which charmed the hearts of the audience," the *Gettysburg Times* reported.

Martha Stallsmith played the part of King Tut.

When it came time for the refreshments, they continued with the Egyptian theme. The *Gettysburg Times* noted that the refreshments included Egyptian salad, Egyptian nut-bread sandwiches and stuffed dates.

When the dance ended at 1 a.m., a group of students had enjoyed themselves so much that they wanted it continue. Eighteen couples drove out to the Graeffenburg Inn near present-day Caledonia State Park. They danced there until 5:30 a.m., had a breakfast of ham and eggs, and then drove back to Gettysburg feeling "dead tired," according to the *Gettysburg Times.*

The Egyptian prom was considered a great success. The *Spectrum* noted that it was "if not the most successful, at least one of the most successful 'Proms' in Gettysburg's history."

26

STATE TROOPER MURDERED IN ADAMS COUNTY

With just five months with the Pennsylvania State Police and only two days at the substation in Chambersburg, Private Francis Haley could still feel a sense of newness and wonder with the job. It was a feeling he would lose all too soon.

Around 2:30 p.m. on Oct. 14, 1924, the report came in to be on the lookout for a lone man in a touring car with New York plates who was wanted as a suspect in the robbery of the Abbottstown State Bank. Upon fleeing the scene, the bank robber had last been seen heading in the direction of Gettysburg along Lincoln Highway.

Around 2 p.m. that day, H. F. Stambaugh, the cashier at the Abbottstown State Bank had found himself alone in the bank enjoying a lull in the busy day. A man had entered the bank wearing a grayish suit and slouch hat, but what alarmed Stambaugh was that he had a red bandanna pulled up over his nose and a pistol.

The robber demanded all of the money in the cash drawer, which amounted to $1,000 (around $13,500 today). He then told Stambaugh to get in the vault. As the cashier walked into the bank vault, he heard something that made him turn around. He saw that the robber had run off.

Stambaugh ran to the bank door. He didn't see anyone on the town square, but he did see a touring car head off down Lincoln Highway driven by a lone man.

The cashier had quickly reported the robbery and the alert had been sent out shortly thereafter.

Private Haley mounted his motorcycle and headed out from the

Chambersburg substation alongside Sgt. Merrifield. They headed east along Lincoln Highway watching the cars around them. As they passed through Fayetteville, Merrifield turned off to patrol along a different road.

Haley knew that the odds of finding the robber so far away from Abbottstown were slim. He had certainly had many opportunities to turn off the highway before reaching Chambersburg. Still, Haley was new enough on the job that the general acceleration of events still thrilled him.

He was driving by the Graeffenburg Inn near the border between Adams and Franklin counties around 3:30 p.m. when he noticed a touring car approaching him from the east. Then he noticed that the car had New York license plates.

The car passed him, but Haley turned his motorcycle around and hurried to catch up to the car. He drew abreast of the car and waved for the driver to stop.

"Pull up to the side of the road and stop," Haley ordered the driver.

Instead, the driver drew a .32 automatic and shot Haley at point blank range. Haley hadn't sensed any danger and hadn't even had time to attempt to draw his pistol. The driver's bullet passed through Haley's right hand and then into his right breast where it also hit his heart before lodging in a rib.

"The momentum of the motorcycle carried the trooper along for a distance of about 25 feet. He then fell off onto the highway, face downward," the *Gettysburg Times* reported.

People sitting on the porch of the Graeffenburg Inn had seen the entire shooting. They rushed to Haley's aid as the car sped off towards Fayetteville.

As the witnesses tried to stop the blood flow, Haley said, "Get that man! I'm shot!"

And then he died; the 11th Pennsylvania State Trooper to be murdered in the line of duty. All of the previous murderers had been captured and the Pennsylvania State Police would make sure that Haley's killer was also caught. His death set off the largest manhunt in Pennsylvania history to that point.

Private Francis Haley of the Pennsylvania State Police. Courtesy of the Pennsylvania State Police.

Largest manhunt in Pennsylvania history

"Today, a bank-bandit and murderer, believed to be one and the same man, sulks in the shadows of whatever he may find to shield him; a criminal hunted like a beast, while more than 100 Troopers seek to avenge the death of one of their comrades," the *Gettysburg Times* reported on October 16, 1924.

Two days earlier, Pennsylvania State Trooper Francis Haley had been murdered when he tried to stop a car that he suspected might have been involved in a bank robbery. He had died on Lincoln Highway just inside the Adams County near Michaux State Forest.

Haley was the 11th state trooper to be killed in the line of duty and Pennsylvania State Police had turned out in force to hunt down the killer.

The killer's car had been found the day after Haley had been killed. The car was found about 5 miles from Fayetteville, burned and abandoned. Though the license plate had been removed, it was still identifiable as the car that Haley had tried to stop and the state police had been searching for as dozens of troopers had combed South Mountain for clues.

Police were also searching for a potential suspect named Gerald Chapman. He had escaped from a federal prison in Atlanta, Ga., and was wanted for murdering a policeman during a robbery attempt in New Britain, Conn.

Meanwhile, the police in Baltimore, Md., had detained a suspect for questioning. He said that his car had broken down near Monterey Pass and he had to take the train to Baltimore.

The *Gettysburg Times* called it the largest manhunt in Pennsylvania history to that point. The Pennsylvania State Police were utilizing just about all of their resources to find the killer.

Amid this turmoil, Haley was buried in the Pottsville Cemetery. It was a reminder to the state police that all of the previous murderers of state troopers had been caught and Haley's killer was still at large.

However, locating the car was a break in the case. The owner of the vehicle was identified as Philip Hartman of Rochester, N.Y. Hartman had also been a former resident of Adams County, working as a farm hand and lineman. The search shifted to locating Hartman. By that evening, the Reading Police reported that Hartman had surrendered to them and confessed to the murder.

He told the police that he had been forced to abandon his car in the mountains when it became stuck in mud. He had tried to hide it by burning it and then set off on foot to Mount Holly Springs. He traveled through the night to reach the town where he caught the train to Harrisburg. He then took a train to Reading.

The Graeffenburg Inn on Lincoln Highway near where Private Haley was murdered. Courtesy of the University of Michigan National Highway Digital Image Collection.

Hartman talked freely while he was in the prison at Reading. He was born in Gettysburg and had later moved to Annville when he had gotten married and then became a father. Earlier in the year, he had traveled to Ohio in search of work. The job lasted only two weeks before he was laid off.

This was the last straw for Hartman and he decided to turn to crime. He stole a car in Columbus, Ohio, and made his way back to Adams County robbing gas stations along the way. Eventually, he found himself in Abbottstown where he decided to rob the bank there.

"My intention was not to kill the state trooper. I noticed him following me in the vicinity of Graeffenburg Inn. I aimed for his shoulder and as I did, he turned. The murder was not deliberate. I just wanted to put him out of the running, so I could make a getaway. After shooting the policeman, I abandoned the car and struck over the mountains," Hartman told reporters.

When he arrived in Reading, he phoned his wife who told him that police had already questioned her and they were searching for him. He had planned to hide out in Reading until things blew over. He would then return home and lead an honest life, but his wife had urged him to turn himself in. Things wouldn't blow over with him having killed a state trooper. Hartman reluctantly agreed and turned himself in.

He would have to throw himself on the mercy of the court.

Cop killer escapes prison, caught and executed

Philip Hartman knew he needed to pay for his crime and that he would have to pay the ultimate price.

"Fight the case? No, I am guilty of the charges. I made my mistake. I am sorry," the 24-year-old Hartman told reporters after he was arrested for murder and bank robbery.

After robbing the Abbottstown State Bank on October 14, 1924, Hartman had shot Private Francis Haley of the Pennsylvania State Police shortly thereafter. Haley had died almost instantly on the highway where he had fallen from his motorcycle, becoming the 11th state trooper to die in the line of duty. Following an intensive two-day manhunt, Hartman surrendered to police in Reading and was returned to the Adams County Jail to await his trial.

Hartman spoke to reporters, "In broken phrases, like a man repenting a wrong deed, struggling in vain with a cigarette that refused to remain lighted," the Gettysburg Times reported. He was unshaven, agitated and weary looking.

The following day state police escorted him as he retraced his route from the time of the bank robbery until he boarded a train to Harrisburg.

At the Abbottstown State Bank, Hartman was taken into the bank and the cashier, H. F. Stambaugh, was asked if Hartman was the bank robber. When Stambaugh reminded the police that the robber had worn a mask, Hartman said, "I'm the man."

Hartman's parents still lived in Annville, but his mother had had a stroke two weeks earlier and was still ill. She hadn't been told of her son's arrest or trial. However, his father and wife did visit Hartman while he was in jail.

Hartman's preliminary hearing was held at the end of October and only Stambaugh and George Johnson, the golf pro at the Graeffenburg Inn where Haley was killed, were called as witnesses to testify.

Hartman had no lawyer to represent him and did not want one. The judge told him that murder defendants needed a lawyer so the court appointed George J. Benner for him. The trial was held in January 1925 and went as quickly as the preliminary hearing. Hartman was found guilty of first-degree murder on January 31.

Following his conviction, Hartman was returned to the Adams County Jail to await his execution. Benner appealed for a new trial, but the appeal was denied.

"Several months' incarceration in the Adams County jail, with freedom of the corridor granted him by Sheriff Shealer, instilled in Hartman desire to escape and he planned with and inveigled Roy Diamond, Annville, boyhood companion of his, to assist him," the *Gettysburg Times* reported.

Diamond had tried to smuggle steel hacksaws to Hartman that he would have used to saw through the bars that covered the cells and windows. Diamond was caught, though, and was soon residing in the same prison as his friend.

As the date for the execution approached, Governor Gifford Pinchot granted Hartman a 30-day respite. This came about due to the efforts of Clyde G. Gleason, a professor of psychology at Gettysburg College, who was seeking a way to stop the execution.

Gleason's last-ditch effort failed. On the morning of November 28, Sheriff Shealer read Hartman his death warrant at the county prison. Hartman and an armed guard then left the prison for Bellefonte and Rockview Penitentiary. On the morning of November 30, 1925, Edgar L. Hildebrand, a Gettysburg College student who had been helping Gleason, and a prison guard escorted Hartman to the electric chair.

Hartman's step did not falter as he walked. "The smile remained while attendants were adjusting the apparatus before the current was applied. Not a word was uttered by Hartman as he was placed in the chair," the *Gettysburg Times* reported.

He was declared dead at 7:09 a.m. He was the 155th person in Pennsylvania to die in the electric chair, which had replaced hanging as a form of execution in 1915.

27

PLAYING A GAME OF "RIDE" AND SEEK

Lester Albright, Leonard Bowling and Wilson Shulte scattered as one of their friends covered his eyes and began counting. They scurried around, searching for a place to hide; someplace they wouldn't be found. Crossing into the freight yards for the Western Maryland Railroad in Gettysburg, the boys climbed into a box car Friday morning, November 21, 1929.

Their hiding spot worked better than expected because they weren't found until Sunday afternoon.

As the boys hid quietly in the box car, a trainman walked by making one last inspection of the train cars. Seeing the open box car, he shut the door and locked it.

Surprised, it took the boys a few moments before they realized they had been locked inside. When they did, they jumped from their hiding places and began banging on the door trying to attract attention. Then the train began moving!

Thus began their 118-mile journey to Cumberland, Md.

Fighting down their initial panic, the boys thought it would be an adventure to take a short ride on the train, but then minutes turned into hours and the hours into days. The train did make one stop in Highfield, Pa., so that the train could be shifted to the main line of the Western Maryland Railroad.

The Western Maryland Railway began as the Baltimore, Carroll and Frederick Rail Road in 1852. It started in Baltimore and was built westward, eventually reaching Hagerstown, Md., in 1872. Within a year after its founding, the company became the Western Maryland Rail Road Company and then later still, the Western Maryland Railway Company.

The company built an extension into Pennsylvania in 1881 and connected to the Harrisburg and Potomac Rail Road in 1886. Next, the Western Maryland Rail Road connected to the Baltimore and Ohio Railroad at Cherry Run, W. Va., in 1892. This connection improved freight traffic on the railroad.

An extension that ran to Cumberland was completed in 1906. From there, the railroad would extend to Connellsville, Pa., and south into West Virginia.

"The first gnawing of hunger over-took the lads Friday evening. It was too cold in the car to sleep either night, and the boys kept awake by moving around," reported the *Gettysburg Star and Sentinel* on November 29, 1929.

On Sunday morning, a surprised trainman unlocked and opened the box car in the Western Maryland train yards in Ridgeley, W. Va. The boys jumped out and asked how to get back to Gettysburg. The trainman turned the boys over to a railroad detective named Hanson. He listened to their story and turned them over to the Salvation Army in Cumberland and notified a detective there named Charles Wilson.

"After eating some hot food and a sleep, the trio were none the worse for their experience," the *Star and Sentinel* reported.

Wilson notified the boys' parents and Levi Albright and John Bowling, fathers of two of the boys, drove to Cumberland to pick up the boys on Sunday afternoon and drive them home.

The families had notified the Pennsylvania State Police when their sons hadn't returned home from playing on Friday, but the police hadn't been able to find any hint as to the boys' whereabouts.

As passenger service declined in the 1950's, the Western Maryland discontinued it altogether in 1959. By 1973, the Western Maryland Railway became part of the Chessie System, which in turn became CSX Transportation in 1987.

28

GETTYSBURG HIGH'S SCARLET FEVER VACATION

While it isn't too surprising when schools close, usually it's for bad weather or a holiday. In 1932, however, Gettysburg High School closed because people were coughing.

Throughout January, Prof. Walter D. Reynolds, the principal of the high school, had seen absenteeism increase. It had reached epidemic proportions by the end of the month

"Each day this week, according to Professor Reynolds, found more and more pupils coughing and sneezing, all on the verge of grippe," the *Gettysburg Times* reported.

When attendance was taken on Jan. 31, more than 50 students were missing. The school enrollment was around 260 students.

"According to Miss Helen L. Cope, supervising principal of the Gettysburg public schools, the percentage of absentee pupils at the High school was greater than any time for the last 25 years," according to the newspaper.

To make matters worse, one member of the senior class was showing signs of scarlet fever. Clare Starner hadn't been in school since the week before, but his younger brother, Charles, had been attending. The fear was that Charles may have been spreading the disease among the student body.

Though scarlet fever is treatable today with antibiotics, in the 1920's, it was a dangerous childhood disease. It is caused by a bacterial infection that showed itself three to seven days after a child is exposed to the disease. The symptoms include high fevers over 100 degrees, a sore throat, headaches, nausea, vomiting and abdominal pain.

A scarlet rash that feels like sandpaper appears on the neck and then spreads to the rest of the body. Even a child's tongue can become red and swollen. The rash will disappear after a week, though the tongue can remain swollen for days longer. As the rash disappears, the skin may peel off.

Gettysburg High School was located at York and Hanover streets in 1923. Courtesy of the Gettysburg Area School District.

According to WedMD, scarlet fever can lead to other ailment such as "ear infections, pneumonia, and serious complications such as kidney problems and rheumatic fever (affecting the joints, heart, and other organs)."

Reynolds consulted with Cope and the Gettysburg Board of School Directors and it was decided to close the school until Monday, Feb. 5. As an indication of how serious the administration saw the problem, the school was closed at 10 a.m. on the same day and the students were sent home.

"Although there are no cases of scarlet fever reported in Gettysburg among school children, it is the belief of local school authorities that closing the High school for several days will afford an opportunity for students to take better care of themselves and guard against an epidemic of that disease," the *Gettysburg Times* reported.

The high school, which was located at the intersection of York and Hanover streets in Gettysburg, was the only school affected by this decision.

"Miss Elizabeth Rummer, principal at Meade building and teacher of seventh and eighth grades, said a wave of pupils at the building last week, but at the present time, the percentage of children absent was not greater than usual," the *Gettysburg Times* reported.

However, the newspaper noted that a week earlier 25 of the 154 seventh and eighth grade students had been absent.

The High Street school reported normal absenteeism.

It appears that the administration's pro-active actions may have headed off a worse problem. In the next couple months, scarlet fever hit a number of other schools in Adams County forcing them to close until the problem had passed.

29

HANOVER REPORTER ON GETTYSBURG ADDRESS GETS HER RECOGNITION

Mary Shaw Leader of Hanover got up early on November 19, 1863, and started off on her walk to work. Hours later, after a cold 15-mile walk, she arrived in Gettysburg to attend the dedication of the Soldiers' National Cemetery. Since the Battle of Gettysburg in July, the cemetery had been laid out and the remains of the soldiers killed in the battle had been reinterred.

She, along with hundreds of other people, stood through U.S. statesman Edward Everett's two-hour-long speech and President Abraham Lincoln's less-than-three-minute speech.

Eyewitness accounts of Lincoln's speech, which would become known as "The Gettysburg Address", have said that initial reaction to it was mixed. Historian Shelby Foote has said that applause was "barely polite." Sarah Cooke Myers, who attended the speech, recalled in 1931, "There was no applause when he stopped speaking." However, the *New York Times* article on the speech said Lincoln was interrupted five times by applause.

When Leader returned to Hanover, she prepared her article for the *Hanover Spectator*, a newspaper owned by her family. Her father, Senary Leader, had started the newspaper in 1844, publishing it until he died in1858. Senary's wife, Maria, had then taken over as editor while Leader served as a reporter. She was one of Pennsylvania's first female reporters.

Leader began her article, "On Thursday last, the 19th of November, 1863, was a great day in the history of Pennsylvania and the entire Union. The battlefield of Gettysburg was dedicated with imposing ceremonies in honor of the great victory which decided of the fate of the Nation."

She included the full text of Lincoln's speech and called it a "remarkable speech." Although the country was still engaged in war and would be for two more year, her view of the Battle of Gettysburg turned out to be prophetic as the battle is seen by many as the turning point of the Civil War.

Mary Shaw Leader

Leader "was the only contemporary newswriter to praise what many consider was the greatest speech ever delivered in the English language," the *Gettysburg Times* reported.

While other newspapers (usually Republican) praised the speech, it's not certain how many of those newspapers had reporters at Gettysburg to hear it firsthand.

Leader passed away in Hanover in 1913 while 15 miles away Gettysburg was celebrating the largest gathering of Civil War veterans ever during the 50th anniversary of the Battle of Gettysburg.

She was buried in Mt. Olivet Cemetery with a small marker.

William Anthony, a job printer in Hanover, had learned his trade from the Leader family. After Leader's death, he learned about his small place in history and felt that it should be recognized with more than a small stone. He began a campaign to raise money for a larger memorial that cost $402 (about $9,500 today).

Anthony also arranged a memorial dedication service patterned after the cemetery dedication services in 1863. Around 600 people attended the service on November 10, 1941. Gettysburg College history professor, Dr. Robert Fortenbaugh, delivered the dedication address. Rev. Dr. Harry Hursh Beidleman, pastor at St. Matthew's Lutheran Church in Hanover, read the Gettysburg Address. The Reformed Emmanuel Church a cappella choir sang a Civil War song and 15-year-old Wirt Crapster, Leader's grand-nephew unveiled the monument.

30

THE PIONEERING COUNTRY STORE IN TABLE ROCK

Being a small country store didn't stop Lower's Country Store in the Table Rock area of Adams County and the Lower and Grim families from bringing new innovations to the county's rural residents.

In 1941, owner C. R. Grim introduced a modern commercial freezer to the store. The *Gettysburg Times* reported that the "installation of the most modern department in the food merchandising field—a freezer-locker plant that will make available more than 100 unit lockers to customers for storing foodstuffs at low temperatures."

The freezer was constructed inside of a 16-foot addition that had been added decades earlier to the store. The room was boxed in eight inches of cork and then lined with a concrete floor and cement-plaster walls and ceiling. Within the freezers were 145 lockers, each with 6.5 cubic feet of space. The lockers could be used by the store or by residents who rented them to use for freezing food.

"Meat or vegetables going into these lockers will be placed first in a pre-freezing unit which freezes them to a temperature of 20 degrees below zero in order to maintain flavors and break down cell structures in meat so that tenderness is increased upon cooking after the storage period," the *Gettysburg Times* reported.

The store had a long history in the county dating back to the mid-19th Century. When the store was first established, it also served as a post office for the area. Samuel Fabor was named the first postmaster for Lower's Mill, which eventually became Table Rock. A mounted mailman delivered mail on horseback once a week to the store where residents would come to pick it up.

Among the innovations that the store brought to the area were:

- Telephones –The store had one of the first three telephones installed in the area in 1887.
- Ice-The store had the first ice house in the area.
- Water-A windmill brought water to not only the store but some nearby residents. "By the use of a huge storage tank located near the store, that water system furnished the supply for water in six homes in the town in addition to the store building," the *Gettysburg Times* reported.
- Ice Cream-H.R. Lower, one of the early owners of the store, made ice cream for sale on Sunday afternoons in the late 1800s.
- Fresh butter-The Hanover Produce operated a skimming station at the store from 1899 to 1915 that produced butter, which was then sold at the store.
- Fresh meats-"In 1949, a slaughterhouse was built and the Lower's Country Store started processing its own meats and turkeys. Livestock is bought locally, and only the best is considered," the *Gettysburg Times* reported.

Lower's Country Store became a center of activity for the area. Not only was it the post office, but it served as a trading post. H. R. Lower also organized the Table Rock Band and an annual picnic at the store that attracted hundreds of people.

For a store that had less than 3,000 square feet of space, Lower's Country Store had a bit of everything: food, tobacco, plumbing supplies, farm supplies and more. The *Gettysburg Times* noted that plug tobacco was purchased by the half ton, locally made crocks were purchased by the car load and thousands of "penny" cigars were sold from the store.

"One fall the store bought 3,000 bushels of shelled hickory nuts gathered under thousands of shellbark trees in the county," the newspaper reported.

The store also sold clothing and material for clothes. The newspaper noted that H. R. especially tried to meet his customer's needs. "He catered to the whims of his customers, meeting the fashions and fads as they came and went," the *Gettysburg Times* reported.

31

COUNTY BOMBS DURING AIR RAID TEST

Early in the morning of June 22, 1943, air raid sirens blared throughout Adams County. People stumbled out of their beds, tripping in the dark because they couldn't turn on any lights. Within an hour, it was obvious that the county had bombed.

The county hadn't been bombed. It had bombed as in "failed."

"If the surprise air raid test early Tuesday morning had been the real thing the amount of damage done in Adams County would have been terrible," a member of the County Council of Defense told the *Gettysburg Times*.

Adams County had been staging air raid drills since the United States had entered World War II, but the U.S. Army had taken over running them in mid-June 1943 and within a week, ran its first drill. The army sent the alert at 4:10 a.m. and the yellow alarm was sounded 15 minutes later. In Gettysburg, the alarm was the undulating sound of the siren on the Gettysburg Fire Hall.

Lights should have been doused and blackout shades drawn all around the county. Instead, people stumbled around in a sleepy daze as the siren became an annoying alarm.

"So realistic was the test, the first sprung by the army, that a number of persons were fearful it was a real raid after they had discovered that the test was in progress," the *Gettysburg Times* reported.

The blue alarm was sent at 4:35 a.m., though it didn't sound until 4:42 because of the volume of telephone calls being made. The only operator on duty at the Gettysburg phone exchange began fielding lots of calls from firemen who wanted to know where the fire was. One of the members of the County Council of Defense said, "The magnificent work of the single operator on duty prevented complete collapse of the local system and allowed the air raid calls to go through."

The hundreds of air raid wardens throughout the county (Gettysburg alone had 179 wardens and 35 highway entrance police) should have been outside by then walking along their streets to make sure no lights could be seen and people had taken cover. Spotters should have been at their station of the roof of the First National Bank looking for enemy aircraft. That wasn't the case. Only a small portion had heeded the alarm.

An air raid spotting station in Biglerville during World War II. Gettysburg had a similar station located on the roof of the First National Bank building.

"A number of county communities did not receive the alarms apparently because sleeping wardens did not hear their phones or failed to distinguish their ring on the party lines," the *Gettysburg Times* reported.

Early morning defense workers had to dress in the dark and couldn't leave their homes in time to get to work.

The all-clear alarm finally sounded at 5:02 a.m., less than an hour after the original alarm had been sounded.

People took a deep breath and began assessing what had happened. New Oxford and McSherrystown hadn't even staged a blackout. When the army took over the air raid drills, the phrasing of how the drill alerts were made was changed. Though it was supposed to be simpler, it turned out to be confusing and so those communities hadn't even realized that they were in the midst of an air raid drill. The county switched back to using the original phraseology a few weeks later.

In Gettysburg, Texas Hot Weiners, Dr. Bruce N. Wolff and the Sweetland Plaza Restaurant were all fined $5 and court costs for not adhering to blackout conditions.

"The test was the most unsuccessful held so far in regards to performance, but it was the most successful in revealing flaws in the system," a Defense Council official told the *Gettysburg Times*.

Another change that was found to be necessary was a new alarm at the fire hall so that the air raid signals wouldn't be mistaken for a fire alarm. On the east side of Gettysburg, the alarm had been confused with factory whistles, adding to residents' confusion.

"That the present differentiation is not distinct enough to make everyone understand immediately that is an air raid alarm was proved all too well this morning. If they raid had been real, the result would have been tragic," the Defense Council official said.

32

LINCOLN'S CHAIR VANISHES

On November 19, 1863, thousands of people gathered in Gettysburg for the dedication of Soldiers' National Cemetery. The keynote speaker of the event was Edward Everett. As his speech continued on and on, people standing in the crowd had to sit or risk their legs buckling. On the stage, the speakers had chairs to rest on until their time to speak came.

President Abraham Lincoln sat in a rocking chair between Everett and Secretary of State William Seward.

"Mr. Lincoln sat on the platform all the time in a rude, little stiff-backed chair, hard, and uncomfortable, but he hardly ever moved," Dr. Henry Jacobs recalled in the *Gettysburg Times* in 1923. He had been a young boy in the audience at the dedication.

When Everett had finished his two-hour speech, the president stood up from his rocker, walked to the podium and delivered 286 words that we still recall today as one of the great speeches of American history.

Today, you can see the chair that President Abraham Lincoln was sitting in when he was killed. You can see the chair he sat in while writing portions of his Gettysburg Address, but as we approach the 150th anniversary of the Gettysburg Address, whatever happened to the rocking chair Lincoln sat on during the dedication ceremony?

That's a tricky question.

Gettysburg College owns it…maybe.

In 1847, Gettysburg College (then Pennsylvania College) students built Linnaean Hall, primarily as a place to display their rock and mineral collections. Over the years, other collections were placed on display in the hall. At first, they were all scientific featuring shells, plants and animals. Then they became historical.

"Miscellaneous collections included coins, Indian relics; natural curiosities, battlefield memorials, and the like. A few stray items such as an ivory cane used by Abraham Lincoln, and a paper signed by George Washington, have also been found," The *Gettysburgian* reported in 1937.

Interior views of Linnaean Hall where the chair Lincoln may have sat in during the dedication of Soldiers' National Cemetery was displayed. Courtesy of Musselman Library Special Collections and Archives.

One of those "stray" items was apparently an armless, cane-backed rocking chair that is supposed to have been the one that Lincoln sat upon during the dedication ceremony for Soldiers' National Cemetery. The problem was there is no record as to where the chair came from. The records may have been lost, damaged or never existed at all. The college did not have the controls that it does now.

This can be seen in the fact that Linnaean Hall had no security for its collections. "The building was open to visitors at all times, and as a result people finally began to steal the valuable collections," *The Gettysburgian* reported in 1937.

The Lincoln chair was apparently a victim of such a theft. When it disappeared from Linnaean Hall in the early 1920's, "No public ado" was made of it, according to the *Gettysburg Times* in 1945.

"College officials knew the chair had disappeared but there was nothing to indicate its whereabouts—and little reason to hope that it might ever be recovered," the *Gettysburg Times* reported.

Linnaean Hall was demolished in 1942 and what remained of the exhibits was moved to the east end of the third floor of Glatfelter Hall, at least the collections that were still around.

"Since there was no place to store the large rock and mineral collections, and geology was taught no longer, they were hauled to a local dump and deposited. As a footnote to this travesty, the October 1, 1942 issue of the *Gettysburg Times* would note that 'The accumulation of junk has been removed, the pigeons and squirrels have found new abodes, the students have no more windows to smash, the Owl and Nightingale Club has no place for its sign, and Joe the Janitor has several hundred square feet more lawn to mow,'" Jay Lininger wrote in his article "Chronicles of Central Pennsylvania Mineralogy" on Pennminerals.com in 1998.

A part of the college's history had been lost, but as the saying goes, "History repeats itself." So it would be with Gettysburg College as the chair that had mysteriously appeared as part of its collections and then disappeared would again just as mysteriously reappear.

Lincoln's chair reappears

For years, Gettysburg College had displayed a rocking chair believed to have been the one Abraham Lincoln used as he sat on the platform during the dedication of Soldiers' National Cemetery where he delivered his Gettysburg Address.

At some point in the 1920's, it disappeared from the collection. No one knew who had taken it or how and no big deal was made of its loss.

Then on April 7, 1945, the *Gettysburg Times* reported, "The little old rocking chair that Abraham Lincoln is reputed to have used on the platform in the National cemetery November 19, 1863, when he delivered his deathless Gettysburg Address, has come back to the sanctuary of the college campus after an absence of close to a quarter century."

The reappearance of the chair was as mysterious as its disappearance and original appearance at the college.

In March, Dr. Henry W. A. Hanson, president of Gettysburg College, received an anonymous letter from Charleston, W. Va., that alerted him that the chair was in Charleston and being offered for sale as a historical object.

The college's lawyer, Richard A. Brown, wrote back to a resident of the city and received a reply from someone who admitted that they had possession of the chair and offered to return it to the college.

"A few days after the letter was received, the carefully wrapped and crated cane-seated rocker arrived at Mr. Brown's office. From there it was sent to the college campus," the *Gettysburg Times* reported.

Who had the chair, how it made its way to West Virginia and the price it would have fetched on the market still remain unknown today. Librarians with Special Collections staff have looked through the papers of the college's past presidents seeking some clue, but have so far found nothing to authenticate the chair.

So the rocking chair with its damaged cane seat and back and scratched wood sits on a wire frame in the college archives. A yellow ribbon is draped from the back to the seat to keep anyone else from sitting on it and a small card is taped to the back of it that reads, "This chair was reputedly used by President Lincoln during the dedicatory services of the Gettysburg National Military Cemetery." This card, which has been on the chair since the college took possession of it, is the only record that the college has of the chair.

The college has no plans at this time to display the chair during the 150th anniversary of the Gettysburg Address.

"We currently have the rocker in storage in Special Collections and not on public display at this time. Without documentation, it would not be fair to display it since we cannot be certain of its provenance. There is plenty more research to be done," said Carolyn Sautter, director of special collections and college archives at Gettysburg College.

The chair is protected in the college's modern archive storage built in 2001. The Special Collections staff also continues to search out more information with the hopes that they will be able prove that not only is the chair the college currently owns the one that disappeared in the 1920's but that it is also the one that Lincoln used in 1863.

If the chair is ever authenticated, it will then be prepared for display such as removing the card and preparing a plaque describing it. Until then, it remains in a historical limbo.

With so many mysteries surrounding the college's early collections, it would be great to be able to solve this one and affirm the chair as a piece of American history.

The chair that Abraham Lincoln is believed to have used during the dedication ceremony for Soldiers' National Cemetery.

33

GETTYSBURGIANS PARTY WHEN WWII ENDS

Late in the afternoon of August 14, 1945, it suddenly became hard to hear someone next to you speaking.

"The fire siren howled, factory whistles blared and auto horns vied with church bells, the fire bell, the court house bell and screaming sirens on the town fire trucks in telling the community that the end of the war had come," the *Gettysburg Times* reported.

On the other side of the world, Japan had surrendered unconditionally and World War II had ended. The Germans had surrendered earlier in the year in Europe. With the six-year-long war ended (America was involved for 4 of them), people wanted to celebrate.

"As the tumult of noise broke forth at 7 o'clock Tuesday evening, homes and stores were emptied as the people streamed into the street—not because there was anything in particular going on there but just to join the smiling, shouting crowd that gravitated toward center square and watched cars speed around the square with horns blowing, motorists waving and cheering but scarcely audible above the hubbub of the sirens and factory whistles," the *Gettysburg Times* reported.

As darkness approached, two young girls rode to the square on their bicycles, which were decorated with red, white and blue bunting. Once darkness fell, other youngsters ran around waving colored flares, where were "the nearest thing to fireworks that could be found in Gettysburg," the *Gettysburg Times* reported.

Police were inclined to let everyone have their fun as long as no one got hurt. They only started to quiet the rowdy ones down as the celebration ticked past midnight and people wanted to get some sleep.

Since word of the victory had come so late on Tuesday, the town had to put off a formal celebration until the next day at 8:15 p.m.

Businesses closed early to allow employees to gather on the square with so many others.

The ceremony was held on the balcony of the Gettysburg Hotel to give the crowd a better view of the speakers. Judge W. C. Sheely was the master of ceremony. The speakers included Rev. Fr. Mark E. Stock from St. Francis Xavier Catholic Church who had also served as an army chaplain during WWI and Chaplain Justus Liesmann who had recently returned from the fighting. Songs were also sung by the gathered crowd or guests.

Area churches also held special services throughout the day to remember those people who wouldn't be returning. Their names and gold stars could be found on the honor roll that had been erected on the south side of the downtown square. According to the *Gettysburg Times*, nearly 4,000 county residents served in the war. Of that number, 118 were killed or died during the war, including 15 servicepeople between V-E (Victory in Europe) and V-J (Victory in Japan) Days. Eight residents were still missing in action by V-J Day and hundreds had been wounded during the war, including 30 servicepeople between V-E and V-J Days.

At the request of President Harry Truman, the country, including Gettysburg, celebrated the end of the war with a two-day holiday that shut down most of the businesses in the town.

34

LIFE IS NOT A BOWL OF CHERRIES FOR COUNTY CHERRY PICKERS

The annual cherry picking season in Adams County is something that came around every year. It had become almost second nature for the growers to project their harvest, set prices to pay pickers and bring in pickers. The beginning of World War II had caused a bit of a shake-up because it became harder to find pickers since many men were in the Armed Forces and women were filling a lot of the jobs typically done by men.

However, 1945 was a season where it seemed that everything that could have happened and growers had to wonder each morning what was going to happen.

The 1945 cherry season started out with bad news for county growers. When the 200 members of the Adams County Fruit Growers Association met in early May they looked at their estimates for the summer's harvest. Cold damage to every area in the county except for the Aspers area was expected to reduce the harvest to one-third of its normal size.

Harvey B. Raffensperger of Arendtsville presided over the meeting. He told the group that the cold freezes had seemed to wander haphazardly through the county. "He told of one orchard in which all of the blossoms had been frozen in on spot while 80 feet away the trees were not harms at all. Most of the freeze damage was done to orchards on low ground, and the fruit trees on hill tops suffered very little, it was reported," the *Star and Sentinel* reported on May 5, 1945.

Still, the remaining cherries would need to be harvested with imported workers. The workers were teenagers who would be bussed in from surrounding counties or even out of state. The growers would make arrangements to house and feed them, but the growers association also set a minimum rate that the pickers could be paid. Though individual growers could pay more to attract workers, they couldn't pay less than the minimum rate. The base rate was the same as it had been in 1944, though demand for workers was likely to mean that few of them would be paid that rate.

The Musselman family: Mr. and Mrs. C. H. Musselman and their children, Lester and Louella. Courtesy of the Adams County Historical Society.

The next month, Elmer Bostwick and G. A. Nahscoll, both with the War Food Administration, announced that the "entire hot packed and frozen red sour cherry crop in the county will be taken by War Food Administration," according to the *Gettysburg Times*.

As the United States had entered World War II, it was obvious that farmers were coming out of the Great Depression. Farm income was higher than it had been since 1929. However, when the U.S. entered the war, the government became more involved in food production and prices in order to support the surging growth of the Armed Forces. The War Food Administration was in charge of making sure that U.S. troops had plenty of food to eat. Farmers were asked to produce more and citizens were asked to consume less and the War Food Administration would contract to buy a portion of an area's or farmer's crops.

Bostwick and Nahscoll told a gathering of cherry growers who met in Biglerville High in June, that their cherries would be baked into cherry pies, which were "one of the greatest morale builders among foods served to the armed forces overseas and in camps and stations in this country."

Though Adams County farmers had received WFA orders in previous years, this was the first time that a blanket order for an entire crop had been issued to Adams County.

It was believed at first that there would still be some cherries available that growers could sell to individual households for home canning or consumption. As the cherries started to ripen, it became obvious that even this small amount of cherries would need to be used to meet the amount that the WPA wanted.

The need for the blanket WPA order was because the cold had damaged so many of the cherry trees in the county.

Picker problems in Adams County

Adams County cherry growers were faced with a third of their normal cherry harvest in 1945. The *Gettysburg Times* reported that "cold weather damage and cherry leaf spot had reduced the crop to 35 per cent of normal and rendered the quality unsuitable for domestic processing and consumption."

This meant that when the U.S. War Food Administration needed cherries for pies to feed to U.S. servicemen, all of the county's cherry crop would be needed to fill the order.

The silver lining to this is that the federal government set the price that it would pay and the government, even in 1945, wasn't known for bargain shopping. At the end of June, the WFA announced that it would pay 13 cents a pound for cherries. This was a significant increase over the 7.75 cent per pound that it paid in 1944. This increase meant that the pickers would be paid more as well. Cherry pickers were to be paid 40 cents for each eight-quart bucket. They were paid 24 cents in 1944.

Despite the fact that cherry pickers in Adams County would be earning premium wages, within a few weeks, growers were wondering whether they would be able to hold onto the workers they needed in order to meet the WFA order.

"Unless Uncle Sam slashes some 'red tape' to make some meat available Adams County is likely to lose several hundred cherry pickers…and that will mean loss of a portion of the already depleted cherry crop," the *Gettysburg Times* reported in mid-July.

The C. H. Musselman Company had brought in 150 youngsters from Florida and Pennsylvania, but found themselves without and meat to feed them. Louella Musselman Arnold had applied for extra food points in order to feed workers, who were housed in the Biglerville auditorium for the summer, Arendtsville High School and Biglerville Grade School. They were needed in order to feed the seasonal workers. Each day the cherry pickers ate breakfast and dinner in the Musselman cafeteria. Their lunches were delivered to them in the orchards each day at noon.

"But when Mrs. Arnold tried to get meat with her extra points she found none available. Her main source of meat supply had been temporarily closed by the OPA for some minor misunderstanding and other meat dealers to whom she appealed declared that they could not supply her additional needs because OPA restrictions limited them to a prescribed quota which was barely sufficient for their regular household trade," the *Gettysburg Times* reported.

Other growers faced similar problems. A meeting with state and local officials was set up and a committee traveled from Adams County to Harrisburg to secure all of the needed permissions and approvals.

"In the meantime Mrs. Arnold is serving the pickers jelly and peanut butter sandwiches, some egg sandwiches and vegetable platters. But the youngsters want some meat," the *East Berlin News Comet* reported.

A new supplier was eventually found, but the ups and downs of the season must have left farmers feeling more exhausted than usual at the end of the season.

Pickers were also having other problems to deal with. In early July, a bus carrying a group of girls back to the home in Dover, Pa., lost two of its wheels while traveling down East York Street in Biglerville. Luckily, no one was injured.

Then a couple weeks later, two busloads of boys from Wilkes-Barre, Pa., were driven into Gettysburg to watch a movie on Saturday night and do a little shopping. These cherry pickers decided to pick more than cherries. Sixty of them were arrested for shoplifted when they returned to board the buses.

"When they started searching the youths there was a wholesale 'delivery' of merchandise to the police," the *Gettysburg Times* reported.

Food production during WWII had proven to be worth the headaches for growers, though they still earned far less than non-farmers. "Between 1940 and 1945, net cash income for farmers increased from $4.4 billion to $12.3 billion. The average farmer went from a net income of just over $700 to over $2,063 – yet farmers still earned only 57 percent of what their urban cousins made," according to Wessel Living History Farm's web site.

35

FREED POW RETURNS HOME TO BIGLERVILLE

Charles Pensyl of Biglerville answered a knock on his door on December 1944 and saw a soldier standing in front of him. The man asked to see the Logan children. The five children of Otis Edward Logan were staying with their Aunt Maude and Uncle Charles. Maude Pensyl was Logan's sister. The army officer told the children that their father was missing in action and believed captured during the first day of the Battle of the Bulge in Europe.

Logan was among the millions of Americans who either joined or were drafted into the Armed Forces during World War II. Despite the fact that he was a married father of five children, he entered the U.S. Army on December 1, 1942.

He trained for nine months at Camp Van Dorn in Mississippi and Camp Maxey in Texas before he was shipped overseas to fight as a "mortar gun operator" with the 99th Infantry, 393rd Division, Company B.

The Logan family waited anxiously in the following weeks wondering whether Logan was alive or not. Then on February 17, 1945, Logan's father, Otis A. Logan, received a card that Logan had written from a German prison camp. He had been captured and was now a prisoner of war.

Logan was sent to Stalag 13C in Hammelburg, Bavaria. The camp had been created in the summer of 1940 when short, wooden barracks were built to house POWs. The first prisoners housed there Belgian and French soldiers captured during the Blitzkrieg of 1940. Serbian, Polish, Italian, British, Russian and American POWs were also eventually housed in the Stalag 13C. Each nationality was housed in separate barracks.

Enlisted men, corporal and below, were required to work while in the camp. They were assigned work groups at nearby farms and facto-ries. After the war, Logan told the *Gettysburg Times* that the food and treatment he received at the camp were "pretty bad."

Stalag 13C Prison Camp in Hammelburg, Bavaria, is liberated in April 1945. Courtesy of Uncommon German Travel.

The Red Cross agreed about the camp conditions. A Swiss dele-gation from the Red Cross reported in March 1945 that prisoners con-sumed only 1050 calories a day about half of what the average person needs. The average temperature in the barracks was 20 degrees Fahr-enheit. Men were sick and malnourished. Morale and discipline were low. "No Red Cross packages had reached the Americans since they started arriving in January. They only reason they didn't starve was the generosity of the Serbian officers, who shared their packages," according to the web site, Uncommon Travel Germany.

In 1945 as the Third Reich crumbled, Gen. George Patton sent a tank force to penetrate the German lines and free the prisoners in Sta-lag 13. "The men of Task Force Baum, as it was called, ran into heavy resistance coming in but they reached the camp on March 24, 1945. The tanks knocked down the fences, but they also started firing at the Serbian officers, mistaking them for Germans," Uncommon

Travel Germany reports.

Things were quickly straightened out and the tanks eventually left with many of the prisoners who were fit to march. "On the way back, the Task Force was ambushed and forced to surrender. Out of the 314 men in the unit, 26 were killed and most of the rest were captured. Most of the POW's returned to the camp as well," according to Uncommon Travel Germany.

The 47th U.S. Tank Battalion ultimately liberated the camp for good on April 6, 1945. Logan finally left the camp on April 29.

"At the time of his liberation the prisoners from Stalag 13C were being evacuated to the rear. Yankee tanks took the guard completely by surprise and they laid down their arms without a fight," the *Gettysburg Times* reported. "Pfc. Logan said that he had his first decent meal of roast beef, mashed potatoes, peas and gravy after liberation, and that he had no personal belongs when he was freed. All had been taken from his by the Germans."

Once freed, Logan received a 60-day furlough and returned to Biglerville to reunite with his family in early June 1945.

Because he had also been injured before being taken a prisoner, Logan also received the Purple Heart for his service.

Logan died on March 16, 1986, at the age of 77. He was living on Middle Street in Gettysburg and died at home. His service was held at the Peters Funeral Home and he was buried in the Biglerville Cemetery.

36

MEDAL OF HONOR PURCHASED FOR A DIME

Hugh Krebs of Chambersburg was a collector so it seemed only natural that he would become an antiques dealer. He could prowl yard sales, flea markets and estate auctions looking for trinkets and treasures that caught his eye.

In 1946, Krebs was "nosing through items," as he put it, that were offered for sale at an auction in Adams County. A box of loose and small items had been set aside because nobody had been interested in them. It was a "junk" box, according to the *Chambersburg Public Opinion*. However, it was also selling for only a dime.

Since he was a general collector and not searching for anything in particular, Krebs rooted through the box to see if it was even worth a dime. Inside, he found a piece of history. It was a 19th Century Congressional Medal of Honor.

Krebs soon found out that even among Congressional Medals of Honor, the one he had found stood alone. "A Congressional Medal of Honor, the only one awarded to a soldier who disobeyed orders in a time of war, ends up in a box of worthless trinkets and junk to be sold for ten cents," Pete Ritter wrote in the *Public Opinion*.

The Medal of Honor that Krebs had purchased for 10 cents had been bought through the preservation of soldiers' lives and a Union artillery line during the Battle of Gettysburg.

On the third day of the battle, Capt. William E. Miller from Carlisle commanded four companies of the Third Pennsylvania Cavalry. He was sick and barely able to sit in his saddle, but he was hoping that he and his men wouldn't be engaged in any fighting that day. Miller's commander had ordered him to hold his position in the woods along Low Dutch Road, southeast of Gettysburg, under any conditions.

From his position, Miller watched as Confederate cavalry began assembling into eight regiments. He could also see what was drawing them together. The Confederate cavalrymen were going to try and break through the Union line to destroy the artillery pieces that were pounding their fellow soldiers engaged in Pickett's Charge.

Medal of Honor Winner William E. Miller

It was possible that they would succeed. The Confederate cavalry greatly outnumbered the Michigan cavalry, which were the only defenders between them and the Union artillery.

"The Michigan cavalry mustered to charge the onrushing sabres of the Confederate horsemen when Capt. Miller, seeing the obvious strategy, turned to his first lieutenant, William Rhawl Brook, asking his support in disobeying the order to hold fast at that point. Brook agreed," Ritter wrote.

Miller led the charge of the Third Pennsylvania. The Confederate cavalry was focused on the Michigan cavalry and didn't see the charge on their flank until it was too late. The Third Pennsylvania split the Confederate line, disrupting the Confederate charge. Rather than a penetrating charge through the Union line, the Confederate cavalrymen quickly found themselves engaged in close quarters sabre battles.

Miller was wounded in the battle with what he laughed off as "a little hole in the arm." Though his role in the action was not mentioned in the official records, it was not forgotten. "In July 1897, the Congressional Medal of Honor was bestowed upon Capt. Miller by President McKinley and presented by Secretary of War Russell A. Alger, who as a colonel in the Fifth Michigan Cavalry witnessed the battle," Ritter wrote.

Miller died in 1919 and is buried in National Cemetery in Gettysburg.

How the medal came to be in a junk box sold at auction is not known. Krebs sought out any descendants of Miller's but didn't find anyone.

Once it became known that Krebs had the medal, different historical societies and the Carlisle American Legion made offers to buy it from him. He turned them all down. Once Krebs learned the story behind the medal, he knew that it was worth more than 10 cents. It was priceless.

37

BURGESS "CUPID" CALLED ON TO HELP

It was a bit early for Valentine's Day, but Gettysburg Burgess William G. Weaver was called on to serve a cupid in January 1950.

He announced at a meeting that he had received a letter addressed to the "Burgermeister" of "Gettysburgh." The letter was "printed in German script," according to the *Gettysburg Times* and was from two women in Hamburg, Germany.

Amelie Schmidt, 48, and Margarethe Lange, 45, wanted to correspond with single men in Adams County. Schmidt wrote that she weighed 170 pounds and Lange wrote that she weighed 155 pounds. Both women said that they were good cooks and housekeepers and they included pictures with the letters. However, since the women only spoke German, any interested male needed to be able to read and write German.

"Through a somewhat sketchy interpretation of it, the burgess deduced that the two women think they would like the United States much better than Germany, and would like to come here," the *Gettysburg Times* reported.

Weaver announced a week later that he had gotten his first "nibble" from a man interested in the "friendship circle." It didn't come from an Adams County man, though. An unnamed Carlisle man called the burgess asking for the names and addresses of Lange and Schmidt.

"Adams county men may be more cautious, or maybe they haven't got around to inquiring yet, but the female of the species has not been backward about expressing opinions," the newspaper reported.

Weaver said that he had also received calls from two women who were outraged that Weaver announced the letter and its contents. Weaver told the newspaper that the gist of the calls was, "We've got enough old maids in Adams county now, we don't need any more."

The mail-order bride industry can trace its roots in the United States to the American West. The number of men in the West far outnumbered the women so it was difficult for men to find themselves wives.

Asian workers would arrange with a mail-order bride service for brides to come from China or other Asian countries to marry them. It was the business version of arranged marriages.

Successful western farmers and businessmen would write to churches and family in the East or ran advertisements looking for wives. The women would write and send pictures and a courtship would take place via mail until the women agreed to marry a man they had never met in person. They were willing to do this as a way to gain financial security and even explore life on the frontier.

The 1950 incident wasn't the first time that the Gettysburg burgess had been asked to help arrange marriages. In the lead up to the 50th anniversary of the Battle of Gettysburg in 1913, a resident of St. James, Mo., wrote to Burgess J. A. Holtzworth in late May. He noted that he and a group of four or five other Missouri veterans were coming to Gettysburg for the reunion. They aged veterans were hoping that the burgess could direct them toward some single women.

The Missourian wrote, "...if you have got a few good widows or old maids who would like to marry and go west, we can accommodate a few. They must be good housekeepers and not too young."

The *Gettysburg Times* reported that the burgess would forward the names and contact information of any women who were interested in applying "for the position of unsalaried housekeeper."

It's wasn't reported whether the burgesses had any success in arranging marriages.

38

FRIENDS IN BUSINESS FOR 50 YEARS CELEBRATE THEIR PARTNERSHIP

When Luther Alleman opened his market on Baltimore Street at the end of the 19th Century, Samuel Spangler saw much of the business for his nearby market dry up. His successful business was suddenly struggling.

"The huge Alleman store was able to undersell the small merchants and Mr. Spangler was among those feeling the pinch," the *Gettysburg Times* reported in 1950.

With no other options in sight, he continued to work to keep his business going. Then one day, he was in the office of Wesley Oyler at his coal yard on North Stratton Street.

"A man from York named Halter also dropped into the office to pass the time of day. Halter was a somewhat flashy man. Mr. Oyler recalls that he wore a huge diamond ring, and had a favorite trick of writing on glass windows to prove that the ring was a genuine diamond," the newspaper reported.

The three men started talking business and Halter said, "We can put up a plant, haul in dead horses and get hides and tallow. The business is all profit."

Spangler was quick to jump on the idea, but Wesley Oyler said that he wasn't interested. After Halter left, Spangler tried once again to interest Oyler.

"If you put up the money, I'll do all the work," Spangler offered.

A few days later, Spangler saw his brother-in-law, J. Price Oyler at a Patriotic Order Sons of America meeting. Unlike Wesley Oyler, J. Price Oyler was interested in the idea. He said that he had farming property that was far enough outside of Gettysburg so that the smell wouldn't annoy anyone and it was close to rail connections. The two young men also decided that there was enough scrap lumber available that they could construct their own building for rendering carcasses.

Rendering is the process of using pressure and high temperatures to convert an animal carcass and/or its byproducts into usable products. It involved mixing, cooking, pressurizing, fat melting, and water evaporation.

The Oyler and Spangler plant on Hunterstown Road in the 1930s. McDermitt Concrete is currently located on the land. Courtesy of the Adams County Historical Society.

Oyler and Spangler decided that they had little to lose in the venture but time.

And so they began collecting carcasses and rendering them to produce hides, tallow, tankage, beef scraps and other items from the bodies.

The business prospered and the following year, the partners bought the old ice plant on Hunterstown Road, which was near Oyler's farm. In 1908, the partnership bought the first truck in Gettysburg to use to collect carcasses.

In 1911, Oyler and Spangler decided that selling tankage (the cooked material left after liquid fat id drained and separated) from the rendered bodies wasn't proving to be a profitable revenue stream. However, tankage contained a lot of nitrogen, which was a vital component in fertilizer.

"Could they not make a fertilizer just as good as any other, and by producing it on the spot not only provide themselves [an additional] business but also provide the farmers of Adams county with an improved fertilizer made locally and easily obtainable?" the *Gettysburg Times* reported.

Business took off again.

Then to avoid hauling products to the railroad, they built a new plant on the south side of Hunterstown Road alongside the railroad tracks in 1915. This plant operated until 1942 when it burned down. McDermitt Concrete is now on the site.

Oyler and Spangler began making insecticides in 1925 and the rendering business was sold in 1930 to a Hanover company. Central Chemical Company in Hagerstown, Md., absorbed the business in 1936, but it continued operating as Oyler and Spangler Fertilizer.

As Oyler and Spangler's partnership grew more and more successful, they became more involved with the community. They built Natural Springs Park for the community and both men were active in the Rotary Club and served as president. Spangler served at the county treasurer for a year and later went on to be the president of the Times and News Publishing Company. Oyler served as the Republican Party county chairman for six years and as an associate judge for eight years.

Oyler and Spangler Fertilizer was one of the largest businesses of its kind in the region and in 1950 the two men celebrated 50 years of being partners in business together. It was the oldest continuous partnership in Adams County at the time.

Sadly, the partnership ended a year later when Oyler died at age 79 on January 23, 1951, from a stroke he had suffered a week earlier. Spangler died from a ruptured abdominal aneurysm on December 5, 1962. He was 88 years old.

39

REJECTED FOUR TIMES, MENCHEY BECOMES A DECORATED VETERAN

Before Francis J. Menchey could fight for his country amid the islands of the Pacific Ocean during World War II, he first had the win the battles against the draft boards at home that didn't want him to fight.

When Menchey graduated from Gettysburg High School in 1943, the U.S. had been at war with the Axis Powers for about 18 months. Like many Americans, the young man wanted to do his part to help his country. Shortly before his graduation, he traveled to Baltimore to try and enlist in the U.S. Navy.

The U.S. Navy rejected him because the physician at the enlistment center said Menchey had a hernia. That was news to Menchey who felt perfectly fine and had never had any indication that he had a hernia.

"Returning to Gettysburg, Menchey consulted his family physician who declared that he was physically fit for service," the *Gettysburg Times* reported.

He tried to enlist locally and was told the same thing. He was unfit because he had a hernia. Then the local draft board called for him to enlist, but he was again rejected for a third time as being unfit.

After graduation, Menchey took a job with Eastman Kodak in Rochester, N.Y., but he didn't give up on his hope of serving in the military. He had the plant's physician examine him.

"There just isn't anything wrong with you," the doctor told him.

So Menchey tried to enlist in Buffalo, N.Y., and was turned down for a fourth time.

When he returned to Gettysburg for Christmas with his family in 1943, he was called up for induction by his draft board again. He traveled to Harrisburg where he was examined and finally, on this fifth attempt to join the military, he was accepted. However, he was told that he would be leaving on January 4, 1944, for army boot camp. Menchey wanted to join the navy. He asked to be reassigned to the navy but he was turned down.

The U.S.S. Princeton burning after she was hit by a Japanese bomb during the Battle of Leyte. Courtesy of the U.S. National Archives.

"He then appealed to a Navy Commander who 'changed' the induction paper after he confirmed Menchey's statements that his Navy enlistment papers of several months previous were still on file," the *Gettysburg Times* reported.

Menchey reported to boot camp at Great Lakes and was then sent to corpsmen's school in San Diego and onto Radium Plaque Adaptomter's school on Treasure Island off San Francisco.

"Six months after his induction Menchey was at Pearl Harbor and a few weeks later he was aboard a task force flagship en route to his first engagement at Angar in the Peleliu group," the *Gettysburg Times* reported.

He also participated in the battles of Leyte, Luzon and Iwo Jima. One time a Japanese bomber strafed Menchey's ship, wounding 17 men and barely missed crashing into the ship.

The Battle of Leyte was a two-month-long battle against the Japanese in the Philippines. It was the first battle in which the U.S. forces faced Japanese kamikaze pilots. Menchey's ship was the acting general communications ship for the attack force. It was under an air attack 85 times in 30 days and general quarters was sounded 149 times during that month. Menchey was part of a medical group of six doctors and 27 corpsmen who took care of the wounded and dying who were brought aboard the ship. At one point, they were caring for 215 men with serious injuries and 375 ambulatory wounded. When the fighting was finished, nearly 53,000 soldiers had been killed.

Menchey was given a month-long leave in early 1945 and returned home to visit his family.

"Rejected three time by the navy and turned down once by draft board examiners Francis J. 'Dick' Menchey, Pharmacist Mate Third Class, is home from the Pacific wars with four battle stars and an extra star for having survived 85 air attacks in thirty days while his ship was laying off Leyte Island, 13 of his 18 months were spent in the Pacific war zone," the *Gettysburg Times* noted.

He was discharged from the Navy in in February 1946. When he returned home, he brought his new wife, Della C. de Baca, whom he had met in San Francisco.

This local hero died in 2002.

40

LIBRARY BECOMES AN ART GALLERY

Who would think to go to a public library to view fine art?

Shortly after the Adams County Public Library moved into the old county jail (the current Gettysburg Borough offices) in 1949, celebrated artist Charles Morris Young donated three of his painting to library.

Young was considered a leading landscape painter in the country in the early 20th Century who had also gotten his start in Gettysburg. He had been born in 1869 on his parents' farm on Taneytown Road about a mile south of Gettysburg. According to the U.S. Department of State, a book about John Constable in Young's father's library sparked Young's interest in art.

"He spent much time sketching and painting in the environs of Gettysburg. To make money, he also carved walking sticks for tourists and sold them as well as watercolor scenes he did of the Civil War battlefields," according to the State Department web site.

As a young man he couldn't afford to attend art school to hone his talent, but he could afford to visit the Walters Collection in Baltimore, which is now the Walters Art Gallery.

He enrolled in the Pennsylvania Academy of the Fine Arts and studied with Robert Vonnoh and Thomas Anshutz, two of the Academy's most-prominent art instructors. It was here that he began to display his artwork, many of which were landscapes of Gettysburg.

He traveled in Europe where his work was also displayed, adding to his notoriety.

"He conducted a studio in the McPherson building, Baltimore street, for several years, about 1897 to 1899, and taught classes of local students in painting," the *Gettysburg Times* reported.

He married fellow artist, Eliza Middletown Cox, in 1903. They

178

traveled to Paris where Eliza enrolled in the Academie Colarossi and Young prepared an exhibition of his paintings for the 1904 St. Louis Louisiana Purchase Exposition. The Youngs would also sometimes show exhibitions of their work together.

Charles Morris Young donated paintings, such as "A Winter Stream" shown above, to the Adams County Library in 1949. Courtesy of Wikimedia Commons.

The Youngs returned to Pennsylvania in 1905 and by 1949, they were living in Radnor.

"Although Mr. Young in his younger days did portraits as well as landscapes and marine subjects and most of his paintings in later years have been devoted to such studies," the *Gettysburg Times* reported.

Young still maintained his connections with Gettysburg, though, and when he decided that he would like a place in Gettysburg to show his work, the new library presented an excellent venue. He donated two scenes along Willoughsby Run and one of the east slope of Culp's Hill that were hung in December 1949.

"He had indicated that ultimately 20 or more of his paintings may be made available to the library," the *Gettysburg Times* reported. "A hope that an interest in art may be stimulated among the youthful visitors to the library also motivated Mr. Young in is initial gift to the library, the [library] board was told."

In January 1950, Young also donated $1,000 to the library to establish a fund for the hanging and care of the paintings and any others that might be added to the collection.

Sadly, Eliza Young died later that year.

"After his wife's death, Charles Young remained in their Radnor home, and had a devastating fire that destroyed more than 300 of his paintings. Tragically, many of them had been returned to the home for the filming by their son, Christopher Young, of a film biography of his father. Titled Nature Is My Mistress, the film is the only visual record of many of those paintings that were destroyed," according to The Magazine Antiques.

Young died in 1964 at the age of 95.

41

SAVING THE CHRISTMAS SPIRIT IN GETTYSBURG

Christmas 1949 was just two weeks past and the new year was still new. Santa had returned to the North Pole. The presents had all been opened and candy canes all been eaten. The downtown Christmas lights had gone dark and the festoons around across the streets had been taken down.

And as the memory of the wonderful community Christmas began to fade, some people wondered if it would ever come again.

The Gettysburg Chamber of Commerce has sponsored the decorating of downtown Gettysburg as it had for many years. In 1949, 110 merchants had donated $533 toward the town's Christmas decorations. The chamber also had slightly more than $80 left over from the 1948 Christmas lights and decoration fund. The problem the chamber ran into was that it had paid out almost $543 by January 1950 for the 1949 decorations and another $247 was still owed.

So decisions needed to be made. First, how was the deficit to be paid? Should the chamber pay it out of its general fund or solicit donations to cover it? Second, should the chamber continue to be responsible for Christmas in Gettysburg?

The chamber members voted not to fund the deficit out of its general fund and instead sought additional donations from businesses that benefited from the additional Christmas traffic in their stores. It was also decided that if the Christmas lights and decorations were to continue, the chamber of commerce would needed a major partner to put on the event.

By the time Halloween rolled around, the chamber of commerce had been seeking donations for the Christmas decorations for weeks.

On Friday, Dec. 1, Glenn Guise, president of the Gettysburg Exchange Club, threw the switch turning on the Christmas lights along

Baltimore, Carlisle, Chambersburg and York streets at 7:30 p.m.

"Lights gleamed red, green and yellow, from thousands of electric light bulbs on the ornamental light standards and from the festoons across the street," the *Gettysburg Times* reported.

Santa Claus arrives on the square in Gettysburg in 1950. Courtesy of the Adams County Historical Society.

The Exchange Club had stepped up to ensure that Gettysburg's community Christmas tradition continued. The club funded the lights, laurel and festooning throughout the downtown while the Chamber of Commerce sponsored Santa Claus and the Gettysburg Christmas tree. Unlike today, Gettysburg used to erect a large, fresh tree on the circle in Lincoln Square. In 1950, the chamber also erected a log cabin beneath the tree with a smoking chimney. A figure of Santa also stood by the cabin door waving to passersby. Beside the cabin a letter box had been placed to collect the "Dear Santa" letters of children.

It must have been filled to overflowing that first night. According to the *Gettysburg Times,* 1,000 children showed up on the downtown square as Santa Claus arrived riding atop a fire truck.

"Kiddies scrambled for the candy he tossed out of his sack in front of the Hotel Gettysburg. Into his ears the youngsters poured forth their Christmas wishes," the *Gettysburg Times* reported.

Christmas in Gettysburg had been saved.

42

THIS JUST IN... A HISTORY OF RADIO IN GETTYSBURG

At 2 p.m. on Sunday, August 27, 1950, Robert Smith, an announcer engineer, pushed a button and the miracle of Marconi came to Gettysburg and the surrounding region. Music was transmitted through the air from a location north of Gettysburg into people's homes miles away.

Though radio had been around since the early years of the 20th Century, WGET Radio became Gettysburg's first commercial radio station.

The first broadcast

The first thing Gettysburgians heard on their radio station was "Stars and Stripes Forever." Then Owen Voight, another announcer engineer for the station, stepped up to the microphone in the main studio and said, "Good afternoon ladies and gentlemen. This is Radio Station WGET signing on its initial broadcasting day WGET transmits on a frequency of 1450 kilocycles, with a power of 280 watts as authorized by the Federal Communications Commission."[1]

The commencement of broadcasting from the station followed a day long open house that saw 3,800 people visit the studio, control room and reception lobby in the small colonial home on Old Harrisburg Road that served as the radio station.

The radio station was, and still is, owned and operated by the Times and News Publishing Company, though it is no longer located on Old Harrisburg Road.

"Words such as—'truth our guide—the public good our aim' and the slogan—'with honor to ourselves and profit to our patrons'—are our inheritance from Robert Harper, our county's first publisher, who founded the 'Centinel in 1800.' These slogans have been and will continue to be the sentiment of every member of the staff of *The Gettysburg Times* and Radio Station WGET," Voight said during his remarks. [2]

Cindy Ford, president of WGET/WGTY, said in an e-mail that she had been told that the editor of *The Gettysburg Times* at the time had started the push for a radio station. [3]

Following a half hour of patriotic music that was meant to allow residents time to locate the new radio station on their radio dials, the dedication program began at 2:30 p.m. For some, it was their first time owning a radio since they hadn't been able to get local news and information before now.

The WGET radio studio was located on Old Harrisburg Road until the mid-1990s. Now it is located on Fairfield Road in Cumberland Township. Courtesy of WGET.

The dedication coincided with a week-long celebration of Adams County's sesquicentennial. Many of the officials and guests who spoke during the dedication program noted that at a time when the Judge W. C. Sheely, president judge of the Adams County courts, gave the dedicatory address on the air.

"Henceforth the voice of Adams County will be more readily heard by many more people in many more localities With this new advantage there is new and greater responsibility May that voice continue to proclaim those things which have made our county great. May it always proclaim the glory of God, faith in America, the value of labor and industry and the principle of liberty and justice of all. To these principles we dedicate this radio station," Sheely said as part of his remarks.

How commercial radio came to Gettysburg

WGET wasn't the first radio station in Gettysburg. That honor belongs to WWGC, Gettysburg College's radio station. Professor Harry F. Bolich was the factory advisor and R. Hartman was the station manager.

However, WGET was the first commercial radio station for the county. It would have to be able to use radio technology to make a profit by attracting both listeners and advertisers at a time when a new communications medium was growing. That medium was television.

I.H. Crouse & Son of Littlestown were hired to build the station and Judge Sheely broke ground for it on April 29, 1950. After the judge turned the first spade full of dirt, Burgess William G. Weaver, Samuel G. Spangler, president of the company; M. C. Jones. Henry "M. Scharf and Attorney Franklin R. Bigham all came forward to turn a spadeful of earth on the new project.

The station was built on 4.25 acres along the Gettysburg-Harrisburg Road with the building being a simple brick structure 44 x 22 feet in size. The Times and News Publishing Company leased the land from the Adams County Institution District for 15 years at a price of $6,405 to be paid in annual installments of $427.

The 310-foot-tall radio tower were made of three steel tubing legs spaced 15 inches apart with welded cross beams. The tower weighed around 7,000 pounds upon completion and was held in place with three sets of four cables. It was painted with alternating bands of orange and white and for night marking there were two 100-watt bulbs glowing at the top of the tower and at two other levels on the tower.

The growth of WGET

From the initial 250-watt station that had a potential audience of 48,000 in 576 square mile area, WGET became a 1,000-watt station in May 1961 with a potential audience of 150,000 in a 1,575 square mile area. Sheely was also on hand to press the button in the press-room of Hotel Gettysburg in 1961 to make that conversion.

"In 10 years and some odd months, WGET has proved its worth and value," Sheely said. "It has grown by leaps and bounds and has rendered the people of this community, and the area it serves, invaluable service in numerous instances, in many respects and in all emergencies."[4]

The birth of WGTY

In 1962, WGET's FM sister station, WGTY, went on the air with 3,000 watts of power. That increased to 10,000 watts in 1969.

"They felt the need for continued news throughout the day. WGET had a news/sports format so the owners wanted to have a music format so WGTY was born," Ford wrote.[5]

Within 20 years, the stations had four towers. The physical size of the station had doubled and the technical equipment in them had quadrupled.[6]

Gettysburg radio today

Over the last 58 years, the WGET and WGTY have served Gettysburg and Adams County as a public forum. Their staff has worked hard to keep the community up to date on emergencies such as storms, fires and school closings due to snow. They have also brought the voices of local newsmakers into listeners' homes.

"WGET, for 20 years, truly has been the Voice of Adams County. It has been successful in its design to be a public forum where the pros and cons of public questions are aired in several community programs that attract thousands of listeners," The *Gettysburg Times* reported at the WGET's 20th anniversary celebration. [7]

WGTY Radio came on the air from a control room on Old Harrisburg Road in Gettysburg, seen here. Courtesy of WGET.

At the same celebration, the Adams County Commissioners issued a proclamation that said, in part, "We feel that in these past 20 years the station has fulfilled its original objective of informing, educating and entertaining Adams Countians from all walks of life." [8]

WGTY's original format was easy listening, but it switched to country music in 1984. Then in 1986, it began broadcasting 24 hours a day.

In 1989, WGTY's signal was boosted to 50,000 watts using a tower in the Pigeon Hills area near Hanover. This not only increased where it could be heard but the potential audience of people who could hear the broadcasts increased to over 1 million.

"This is a very big step for us, and an important change for WGYT," said Rod Burnham, general manager at the time. "It will give the station a city grade signal in both York and Harrisburg."[9]

Both stations continue serving the region today and are among only a few radio stations nationwide that are owned by a company that also owns a newspaper.

WGET is the 1320 AM news, talk and oldies music. It has also been a Philadelphia Phillies Baseball affiliate for many years. Ford said she was proud of the number writing awards the WGET news team has won.[10]

WGYT is the FM station at 107.7 and currently has 16,000 watts of power. It plays country music and broadcasts NASCAR racing. It is also the number one radio station in the York-Adams market. [11]

The current studios for both stations are located at 1560 Fairfield Road next to the offices for *The Gettysburg Times*.

---

[1] *Gettysburg Times*, September 2, 1950.

[2] *Star and Sentinel*, September 2, 1950.

[3] December 2, 2008 e-mail with author.

[4] *Gettysburg Times*, August 28, 1970.

[5] December 2, 2008 e-mail with author.

[6] *Gettysburg Times*, August 28, 1970.

[7] Ibid.

[8] Ibid.

[9] *Gettysburg Times*, January 28-29, 1989.

[10] December 2, 2008 e-mail with author.

[11] December 2, 2008 e-mail with author.

43

ADAMS COUNTY SESQUICENTENNIAL

On a hot evening in July 1948, a group of Adams Countians met in a room that was made even hotter by the presence of so many people. The air conditioning was cranked up and everyone got down to the business of planning a celebration of Adams County's sesquicentennial. The committee had been formed at the suggestion of the Adams County Historical Society.

"Anniversary celebrations are both entertaining and informative," wrote Leighton Taylor, chairman of the Adams County Sesqui-Centennial Association. "They promote good will and fraternalism, encourage enterprise and initiative, and create a just and pardonable pride in progress and achievement. Moreover, with subversive elements trying to destroy our American Way of Life, we need a revitalization of our patriotism and love of country. This we think can be done most efficiently by reminding Adams Countians, in dramatic and colorful presentations, of their free institutions, their exalted and favored position as American citizens, and of the unparalleled progress made by them and their forebears during the County's 150 years."

Brothers of the Brush

With two years of planning, Adams Countians began noticing something different during the summer of 1950. "The rumor that there is a razor blade shortage was spiked Tuesday. ... beards, goatees, mustaches, and sideburns have begun to sprout on manly countenances as countians join in the spirit of things by permitting the facial hair to grow freely," the *Gettysburg Times* reported on August 5th.

The men had joined the "Brotherhood of the Brush" in preparation for the county's 150th birthday party. The men had agreed not to shave their beards for a month. At the end of the celebration, prizes would be awarded for most-luxuriant beard, best full-face beard, blackest beard, reddest beard, grayest beard, most-typical beard and best old-time costume with matching beard. A special award was also given for the man who tried his hardest to grow a beard and failed.

Harold Ecker was a young man in his 20's at the time of the celebration. Besides participating in some of the events during the sesquicentennial, he was also a Brother of the Brush.

"I went to Atlantic City while I was growing a beard and someone wanted to know if I was a Jewish rabbi," Ecker said. He eventually won second place for the reddest beard.

The Brothers of the Brush paid 50 cents for a badge that explained why they weren't shaving. Shaver's permits were also sold for $1 that gave them permission to shave. During the sesquicentennial celebration a Kangaroo Court was also set up to fine any male who was caught shaving without a permit.

The 50 participants showed up at the county courthouse on September 2 to have three Gettysburg barbers judge their beard-growing efforts during August. Some of the men had trimmed their beards in unique ways or added large rubber noses or other features to their faces. More than 2,000 people showed up to watch the judging. "So large was the audience that it nearly overwhelmed the 'Brothers of the Brush' and the judges and practically blocked traffic on Baltimore Street," the newspaper reported.

While the whole thing was a fundraiser for the sesquicentennial, it was also fun for the participants and even the barbers.

"Barbers had a 'field day' harvesting the Brothers of the Brush following the parade Saturday," the newspaper reported. "Most in mock seriousness asked the bearded contestants how long they had been growing the beard, asked how often they shaved, and then threatened to charge 50 cents for each and every shave that had been missed. All finally settled for 50 cents for one shave."

The program from the Adams County Sesquicentennial pageant in 1950. Courtesy of
the Adams County Historical Society.

The Parade of Progress

The sesquicentennial celebration covered five days with each day
filled with events and having a different theme. "Adams County's
biggest birthday celebration ever came in its 150th year," the *Gettysburg Times* noted in 1975.

The party began on Wednesday, August 30 with Queen's Day.
The other days' themes were: Patriotic Day, Youth Day, Adams
County Day and Freedom of Religion Day. Each day, other than
Freedom of Religion Day" featured its own themed parade.

The festivities began on Wednesday, August 30 at 10 a.m. with
an "aerial bombardment" as the program described it. Everyone on

Adams County was encouraged to blow whistles and honk car horns. Churches range their bells.

More than 10,000 people turned out to watch the "Parade of Progress" on Saturday, September 2. It was billed as one of the largest parades in the county's history with 34 floats "representing practically every possible scene in the county's history," according to the Gettysburg Times. Old cars, buggies, costumed participants and 14 bands and drum corps also participated in the parade.

"Back then, we had some beautiful floats in the parade," Ecker said.

The Littlestown Rotary Club won the $100 top prize for the best float. "The wigged and costumed persons on the float danced the minuet while others played the harpsichord and violin as the float passed the judges' stand on Lincoln Square," the newspaper reported.

The Gettysburg Exchange Club won second place with a four-unit float that portrayed the history of Adams County including Mr. and Mrs. James Getty following up in a buggy. Lincoln Logs placed third with a replica of a log cabin on their float with Bernard Fraser playing Abraham Lincoln.

Roland Kime participated in the parade with the Senior Extension Club. "We were on the bed of a truck square dancing," Kime said. The Senior Extension Club also performed square dancing demonstrations throughout the celebration.

Things were so busy on Saturday night that the newspaper report noted that it took 45 minutes to drive through town.

Freedom's Frontiers

The keystone event of the celebration was the performance of "Freedom's Frontiers." It was an original 20-scene theatrical performance that featured a cast of 500 in historical costumes acting out the history of Adams County. It also featured ordnance supplied by Letterkenney Army Deport. The show played four nights of the celebration. Each performance filled the Gettysburg College stadium.

George Sipes was a sixth-grade student living in East Berlin who also played one of the 16 students in an early classroom scene in the pageant.

"We just sat in a classroom and didn't say a word," Sipes said.

"We never even got to see the play. As soon as we were done, we got in a car and left."

Sipes said that Archie Himes, the man who played the teacher in his scene, knew the boys from around town and sports games. He gathered them together one afternoon and asked, "Who wants to be in a play in Gettysburg." A few of the boys raised their hands and they were immediately cast. Luckily, they also didn't need to do any rehearsals for their part either.

Donald Ullery, executive secretary of the Adams County Sesqui-Centennial Association, wrote after the celebration that "a large, curious group of people gathered to witness the display."

Other events

During the days, visitors could walk the main streets of most of the towns in the county and view historical displays in business windows. The businesses were competing for prizes and Thomas Brothers Department Store in Biglerville won the top prize. The display "contained authentic items of a country store of many years ago, according to the judges," the newspaper reported. You could see a pot-belly stove with a live cat sleeping next to it as well as a cracker barrel.

You could also watch historical vignettes performed in various towns. Ecker's wife and daughter dressed in costume to perform in one near the St. James Lutheran Church in Gettysburg. He said that they performed every three hours or so during the day.

Children and adults could enjoy midway games and sports at Gettysburg College.

Visitors purchased wooden nickels that could be used as cash during the celebration, but apparently none of the 10,000 wooden nickels that had been sold were ever redeemed.

44

WITCHES IN
ADAMS COUNTY

Ghosts and ghost hunting in Gettysburg are a cottage industry, but Adams County has also had its share of witches, according to local folklore.

Frank Eckert was life-long resident of Adams County who died in 1960 at age 89. Two years prior to Eckert's death, Don Yoder recorded the stories of witches and witchcraft in Adams County with which Eckert was familiar. Yoder said that he believed that they were the first recorded folk tales of Adams County.

"We have them in other words from a believer rather than in the truncated versions we get from the family, to whom they are no longer important," Yoder wrote in the Summer 1962 issue of *Pennsylvania Folklife*.

Here are just a couple of the tales.

Eckert and a neighbor went to see a male and female pair of hogs that were offered for sale in the Gettysburg Times. Eckert agreed to pay the old woman who lived north of Gettysburg $45 for the pair.

The woman agreed to accept a three-month bank note for the purchase, knowing that she wouldn't receive the full purchase price for three months. If she took the note to the bank prior to the due date, it would be paid at a discounted rate. Eckert signed the note and took his hogs home.

However, about a week later, the old woman showed up saying that she needed payment in full now and not in three months. Eckert told her that she would have to pay the discount for early payment on the note.

"She wanted me to pay the discount or give her a pair of pigs when this sow had pigs," Eckert said.

He told her that wasn't going to happen and that she would have to abide by the terms of the note.

"I'll put a spell on your for 48 months, if you don't give me the money," the woman told him.

Eckert didn't back down and the woman left. Soon thereafter, Eckert had a mare that foaled, but he couldn't get the foal to drink and it finally died. Then the sow he had purchased had a litter of pigs and they wouldn't drink either.

"Whenever they'd go to drink, their head would start to fly around and they couldn't take ahold of the nipple," Eckert wrote.

Desperate, Eckert went to another witch in Hanover. He called her a witch doctor not because of the way she practiced witchcraft, but because she was known to counter the curses that other witches made. Eckert asked the witch for a counter curse. The witch asked for a picture of the old woman who had sold Eckert the hogs, but Eckert didn't have one. He did describe the woman. The Hanover witch recognized the woman from Eckert's description.

Eckert didn't say whether the woman was able to cast a counter curse, but he was forced to sell the mare because she started to act as if she was afraid of him.

In another instance, Eckert said a witch lived in Hunterstown. This witch visited Eckert's grandmother. She walked down to his grandmother's pig pen and walked along the edge.

"She picked up a corn-cob and she stroked them over the back, both of these hogs," Eckert wrote.

That night both hogs took sick and they were dead by morning.

A third witch who Eckert knew of was imprisoned in the county jail in Gettysburg or was she?

Eckert wrote, "She said if she had the blood of a calf, she could go through any keyhole, or knothole, no matter where it was. So they had her penned in jail in Gettysburg for some cause. I don't know what. But the old lady was home every night with her children. And before sunup she was back in jail."

So, apparently, the woman must have found some calf's blood.

45

GETTYSBURG'S FALLEN
IN VIETNAM

On May 28, 1965, a helicopter carrying Capt. Millard Russell Valerius took off from Bien Hoa Air Base in South Vietnam. Valerius had been in-country for just over seven months, having started his tour of duty after serving as an ROTC officer at Gettysburg College.

Valerius' helicopter was between 50 and 100 feet above the ground when it collided with another helicopter.

"One ship burst into flames at the impact and the other appeared to break up in the air, then caught fire,"   reported The *Gettysburg Times.*[1]

Everyone aboard Valerius' helicopter and three of the men on the other helicopter died in the accident. Eight of them died outright in the crash. Two others died of injuries later at the base hospital. One soldier was injured and recovered.

"First reports said that one of the helicopters was returning from Saigon with a crewman who had been injured several days ago in the foot by a Viet Cong bullet He was returning to his unit. The other ship reportedly was leaving the helicopter pad outside the Vietnamese 3rd Corps Headquarters," reported the newspaper.[2]

The deaths were listed as accidental and not due to hostile action.

Learning of the loss

Phyllis Valerius, Valerius' wife, learned of her husband's death three days later. By then, she was living in Missouri, since her husband no longer served at the college. Valerius also had also left behind a son, Michael, 11, and a daughter, Vicki, 9, who would grow up without their father.

"I learned of Capt. Valerius' death the evening of August 13,

1965 when I boarded the ship in Oakland Army Terminal, with my unit, to sail to Vietnam. I had thrown the Gettysburg College quarterly magazine in my duffle bag as the last thing I had packed before leaving with my unit from Ft. Knox, Kentucky. The magazine contained his obituary. He had died, as noted, in a helicopter crash in Bien Hoa, RVN. As a young Lieutenant with a new command heading for Vietnam, I felt a deep loss that night, and do so to this day. I 'visit' Capt. Valerius at The Wall each time I am in Washington, D.C., and thank God I had the honor to serve under him as a student cadet," J.C. Sims wrote about Valerius.[3]

During his time at Gettysburg College, Valerius taught tactics and communications to Gettysburg College union in the ROTC program. He was also the Phi Kappa Psi advisor fraternity. However, he also remained an airborne ranger and a member of Special Forces.

"Capt. Valerius was the epitome[e] of an officer and a gentleman. He was an inspiration to all of us in and a gentleman. He was an inspiration to all of us in ROTC, and his knowledge of tactics, while taking us on Ranger patrols at Indiantown Gap, Pennsylvania, gave us many added advantages during our ROTC summer camp experience," Sims wrote. [4]

Before coming to Gettysburg, Valerius had been stationed at Fort Benning, Ga., with the Infantry Career School. He was born in Benton, Ill. He had a B.S. degree in economics from the University of Illinois. He was in military service for a year after his high school graduation and a year after his college graduation in 1952, but he went active duty in 1958.

Part of the wall

Valerius was buried in Arlington National Cemetery at the request of his wife, but his name is also on the Vietnam Veterans Memorial Wall in Washington, D.C.

Valerius' son, Michael, who was 11 at the time of his father's death, left a message about his father on a web site dedicated to the memorial in 2001. "So plain for one who gave so much," Michael wrote and then went on to give more details about his father. [5]

The Memorial Wall is made up of two black granite walls that are

75 meters long. They sink into the ground with the earth behind them. The tallest point, where the walls meet is 3 meters high and the walls taper to the height of 20 centimeters.

The designer, Maya Lin, felt that "the politics had eclipsed the veterans, their service and their lives." She kept the design elegantly simple to "allow everyone to respond and remember." [6] The names of servicemen either killed in action or missing in action are inscribed on the wall in chronological order of how they died. Currently there are 58,249 names on the wall, though that number can change every Memorial Day if the Department of Veterans Affairs receives new information, according to the National Park Service.

Among the names are 15 men who called Gettysburg home; two sailors, six soldiers, one airman and six marines.

- Specialist Joseph W. Blickenstaff, Jr., Littlestown (U.S. Army, 11th Armored Cavalry) – His tour began on October 22, 1969. He was killed on December 19, 1970 in Binh Duong, South Vietnam.
- Specialist Larry Thomas Brent, Gettysburg (U.S. Army, 77th Field Artillery) – His tour began on May 2, 1967. He was killed on January 16, 1968 in Hua Nghia, South Vietnam.
- Warrant Officer Charles Arthur Businda, Ortanna (U.S. Army, 119th Aviation Company) – His tour began on March 18, 1970. He was killed on April 19, 1970 in Pleiku, South Vietnam.
- Lieutenant Raymond Ellis, Gettysburg (U.S. Navy, 27th River Assault Group) – He served 16 years in the navy. He was killed on September 30, 1965 in Dinh Tuong, South Vietnam.
- 2nd Lieutenant Larry Leroy Hess, Gettysburg (U.S. Army, 5th Cavalry Regiment) – His tour began on August 19, 1965. He was killed on November 17, 1965 in South Vietnam.
- Corporal John Charles Holoka, Gettysburg (U.S. Marine Corps, 5th Regiment) – He served four years in the marines. He was killed on July 22, 1966 in Quang Tri, South Vietnam.
- Lance Corporal Robert Lester Kessel, Gettysburg (U.S. Marine Corps, 4th Regiment) – He was killed on March 20, 1967 in Quang Tri, South Vietnam.
- Private First Class John Russell Miller, Gettysburg (U.S. Marine Corps, 1st Regiment) – His tour began on January 8, 1971. He was killed on January 30, 1971 in Quang Nam, South Vietnam.

- Staff Sergeant Ralph Burton Mitchell, Gettysburg (U.S. Army, 2nd Field Artillery) – His tour began on April 10, 1969. He was killed on August 7, 1970 in Binh Duong, South Vietnam.
- Private First Class John Franklin Riegel, Gettysburg (U.S. Marine Corps, 5th Regiment) – His tour began on July 25, 1967. He was killed on December 19, 1967 in Quang Nam, South Vietnam.
- Private First Class Gary Wesley Runk, Gettysburg (U.S. Army, 1st Regiment) – His tour began on September 26, 1967. He was killed on January 5, 1968 in Quang Tin, South Vietnam.
- Lance Corporal Gerard Jude Sanders, Gettysburg (U.S. Marine Corps, 1st Regiment) – His tour began on August 16, 1967. He was killed on July 5, 1968 in Quang Tri, South Vietnam.
- Aviation Boatswain's Mate Handling 3rd Class Richard Martin Sietz, Gettysburg (U.S. Navy) – He served two years in the navy. He was killed on July 29, 1967 in North Vietnam.
- Technical Sergeant Gerald Allison Snyder, Biglerville (U.S. Air Force, 405th Tactical Squadron) – He served 18 years in the air force. He was killed on May 16, 1965 in Bien Hoa, South Vietnam.
- Lance Corporal Michael Clair Thomas, Arendtsville (U.S. Marine Corps, 5th Regiment) – He was killed on October 17, 1966 in Quang Tri, South Vietnam.
- Like Valerius, the following men were alumni of Gettysburg College before serving and dying in Vietnam:
- Corporal Edgar Brower Burchell, III, Mamaroneck, New York (U.S. Marine Corps) – He was in the marines for three years. He was killed on June 4, 1966 in Quang Nam, South Vietnam.
- Captain Joseph Patrick Murphy, Long Beach, California (U.S. Marine Corps) – He was in the marines for six years. He was killed on March 24, 1967 offshore in Military Region 1, South Vietnam.
- 1st Lieutenant Charles Henry Richardson, Bergenfield, New Jersey (U.S. Air Force) – His tour began on March 18, 1968. He was killed on October 8, 1968 in Khanh Hoa, South Vietnam.
- Specialist Stephen Henry Warner, Skillman, New Jersey (U.S. Army) – His tour began on March 21, 1970. He was killed on February 14, 1971 in Quang Tri, South Vietnam.

Honoring the fallen

More than one million names, including Valerius, were encoded on microchips and launched into space on the Stardust spacecraft. The spacecraft's mission was to collect comet particle dust, but the collection of the names, "provided a way to honor individuals by enabling them to be associated with mankind's most advanced technological endeavor and to be part of the quest of the human species to reach for the stars," according to NASA.[7]

The spacecraft completed a seven-year, 3-billion-mile journey to collect particles from the comet Wild 2. Stardust flew within 150 miles of the comet to collect the particles in January 2004.

Stardust was launched on February 7, 1999. The spacecraft had two sets of microchips. Each set of chips included the same names, including all of the names of veterans on the Vietnam Veterans Memorial Wall. One set of chips returned with the sample return capsule when on January 15, 2006. The other set of chips is mounted to the spacecraft body and will remain in space.

---

[1] *The Gettysburg Times*, May 29, 1965.

[2] *Ibid.*

[3] *www.footnote.com*

[4] *www.footnote.com*

[5] *Thewall-usa.com*

[6] *www.nps.gov/vive/*

[7] *www.jpl.nasa.gov*

46

A DAY IN THE LIFE OF RICK FULTON, DINOSAUR HUNTER

Rick Fulton sees dead creatures where other people see nothing.

Walking carefully along a slope of red shale, Rick moves slowly and keeps his head down. A light rain falls, making the shale slick, but that's not why he moves so slowly. His ability to see dead creatures is not paranormal. It's a trained observational skill.

He stops and points at the ground. "Right there. That white line. The rain makes looking for calcified fossils in red shale easy," Rick says.

Rick is an amateur paleontologist whose prehistoric searches led to the first early dinosaur-age vertebrate fossils found in Gettysburg.

He squats down to get a closer look at the potential fossil find and runs his finger along it. If he likes what he sees, he'll mark the spot so that he or his life partner Cathe Curtis can come back later and excavate it. Right now, he's just searching for the telltale signs of fossils or preserved tracks.

"You learn to lock on patterns," Rick says. "You eventually know the rock so well that even minute changes stand out to you."

Rick has been collecting fossils since he was 14 years old. He liked to walk along the shore of the Chesapeake Bay searching for sharks' teeth and interesting shells. One day, he picked up what he thought was a plant stuck to a shell. It turned out to be a fossilized sponge attached to a fossilized scallop shell. He took it to the Smithsonian Institution and was told it was a previously unknown species of prehistoric sponge.

Rick shifted his searches from sharks' teeth and shells to fossilized bones. As his collection of fossils grew, he began to display his finds at gem and mineral shows.

"My fossils were so well preserved that paleontologists demanded I take them out of the case so they could make sure they were real," Rick says.

Over the years, Rick's finds have found their way into the Pennsylvania State Museum in Harrisburg, the Los Angeles Museum of Natural History, the Field Museum in Chicago and the Smithsonian Institution.

Before he could graduate high school and venture off to college to study paleontology, he decided to pursue another love, his music. Rick had spent a lot of his youth as a guitarist for garage bands, but he decided to chase his recording dream with a surf band, the Nautiloids. Even that constantly reminded him of what he chose to leave behind—nautiloids are a prehistoric mollusk.

"They are basically a shell relative of the squid and the octopus. Yet, this timid sea animal seemed a relentless survivor, having even survived several mass extinction periods, including that which had eliminated the dinosaurs, and their greatest marine competitor—the Ammonoids. It seemed an appropriate name for a proposed young, inexperienced group of soon-to-be (or at least "wanna be") musicians about to begin the upstream swim against the many obstacles one encounters along the path of achievement in the entertainment industry," Rick said in an interview with the Lance Monthly in 2002.

The Nautiloids recorded two songs, Nautiloid Surf and Nautiloid Reef and saw some success in the Maryland, Delaware and Eastern Virginia area before they merged with another band.

Rick returned to school getting his GED, then his associate degree in journalism and bachelor's degree in geography.

He moved to Adams County in 2004 so Cathe could be close to her hometown. He worked as an editor for The Emmitsburg Dispatch, but, during his free time, he would explore the area looking for fossils.

After he wrote an article about fossils a quarry at the north end of Emmitsburg, Maryland, where dinosaur fossils had been found, he got a request to examine some fossils at a farm in Rocky Ridge, where the owner believed dinosaur tracks might have been found.

Rick, who by this time had become a scientifically published, lay-professional paleontologist, jumped at the chance. He wasn't disappointed. He asked permission to begin studying the farm for other evidence of its prehistoric past. Since 2004, his search has yielded thousands of reptile tracks, skin impressions and bones, millipede and insect tracts, plant fossils, and fossil freshwater shrimp and fish. It is the largest early dinosaur-age fossil site ever found in Maryland and has been formally designated "The Fulton Site" by the scientific community.

On this particular day, it's uncertain as to whether he and Cathe will find anything new or what the quality of those finds will be.

He had decided on the search area by looking over survey and topographical maps of the area to try and find potential spots where fossils might have been preserved. Once he marked a few, he overlaid a road map to see if any of the spots had road cuts made through them. Road cuts and stream cuts uncover the deep buried earth to give a paleontologist a snapshot of the different layers of earth at that point.

"You follow the road cut and see where it goes, because it will give you a good idea if there's something there before you approach a property owner about digging on their land," Rick says.

When it's not raining, the other good time to search for fossils is early morning or late afternoon.

"You need the sun to be angular to the ground to create shadows that help you see the fossils better," Rick says. That was the time when he discovered his dig site in Gettysburg.

Rick took a job with the Gettysburg Times in 2007 and went on location to write a story about graffiti. While standing in a stream in town looking at graffiti, he noticed something in the rocks at his feet. He bent down to look closer and found tiny three-toed impressions in the rock...fossil tracks.

He returned to the site later and began further study. Eventually Sarah Principato, assistant professor of environmental studies at Gettysburg College, and William E. Kochanov, senior geologist with Pennsylvania Department of Conservation and Natural Resources, came to study the site.

Kochanov discovered a five-inch jaw section in sandstone in the bank of the creek while searching for additional tracks. Rick also found some rib sections.

"You think these places have been studied for 200 years that everything should have been found, but we are still finding stuff," Rick said.

Dr. Robert Sullivan of the State Museum in Harrisburg made an identification from the jaw section, which had 10 teeth sockets. It is from a giant Late Triassic Period amphibian called at Buettneria. This was a six-foot-long prehistoric 215-million-year-old cousin to today's frogs and salamanders.

Rick theorizes that when the amphibian died, its body washed onto a sand shoal, which would have been in a much larger river. The soft tissues eventually decayed leaving the bones, which were then bleached and scattered on the shoal.

The bones were then covered in sand and fossilized hidden from the elements until erosion brought them back to the surface.

Since the initial find, additional bone fragments have been found that help add to the picture of the amphibian.

"It all comes out like little pieces of a puzzle," Rick says.

While the bones are believed to be from an amphibian, the tracks are from a smaller reptile.

One of the things that Rick has found beneficial, particularly in a historic area like Adams County, is that a broad knowledge of history can be as beneficial as prehistory.

"You don't want to disturb a potential archeological site to get to a prehistoric bone," Rick says.

Once Rick has looked the red shale over, he returns to his marked sites and chooses one that Cathe is not working on. He settles down beside it and opens his tool bag. First, he uses some fine-cut tools to chip away at the surrounding rock to gauge the extent of what he's found. It's a small calcified bone of some sort.

Next, he'll use his hammer and chisel to remove the piece. Then he'll take it back to his house where Cathe will clean and prepare the sample. Good pieces will go off to a museum or into Rick's collection. Poorer-quality pieces will be sold.

Currently, Rick and Cathe have three active dig sites in Adams County. Their attention alternates between the three depending on the weather conditions and what they are finding in each one.

However, Rick is always looking for additional places to explore and dig in to find another clue to the area's prehistory.

Some Pennsylvania sites for fossil hunters

These Pennsylvania sites are listed at *www.suffolkgem.com*:

- Beltzville State Park (Franklin Township and Towamensing Township) – Pennsylvania allows fossil collecting in designated areas in some of its parks. The man-made lake is on a Devonian fossil bed. Fossils can be found by wading and search the rocks under foot.
- Swatara State Park (3 mi. west of Pine Grove) – The Suedeburg site is along an old state road. The road cut exposes the Mahantango Formation.

47

THEY WERE GOOD FOR WHAT AILS YOU

With all the speculation on what the future of health care will look like in the United States, how did it look in the past at least in Adams County?

Being a doctor in the 1700's and 1800's required more common sense and experience than school time. Many doctors in the county practiced medicine without a degree or medical school training.

"Scanning the records of soldiers from Adams County who served in the Civil War brings to light many items of interest on the early medical men of the area, including the fact that a man listed as a physician of that time might have been only a student in high school," the *Gettysburg Times* reported in a 1950 article.

Even those doctors who did attend medical school didn't undergo the rigorous training that today's doctors do. One of the county's early doctors, David Horner of Gettysburg, received his M.D. degree after completing only two five-month-long programs at Washington Medical School in Baltimore.

While some doctors may not have had school training, a popular way of learning medicine was to work as an assistant to a practicing doctor.

"Despite the fact that not until 1881 did Pennsylvania require the M.D. degree for practicing medicine (and those in service for ten years previously were exempt from this requirement), county doctors kept countians in reasonably good health," Robert L. Bloom wrote in *A History of Adams County, Pennsylvania 1700-1900*.

Unlike other professionals who tended to cluster closer to the larger population centers in the county, doctors were spread throughout Adams County. Reily's Directory lists 59 doctors in Adams County in 1880, which was one doctor per every 560 residents, according to Bloom.

"In 1880, three druggists in Gettysburg and two each in Little-stown and New Oxford dispensed pills and bottled and packaged nos-trums. Many people, however, tended to rely on home remedies or purchase the widely advertised patent medicines offered," Bloom wrote.

Dr. Robert Horner of Gettysburg was one of the county's doctors during the 19th century. He helped treat the wounded after the Battle of Gettysburg. Courtesy of the Adams County Historical Society.

Ailments were either treated in the doctor's office or in the patient's home. If patients needed hospital care, they had to travel out of county until the early 20th Century.

The closest thing to a hospital in the county at the time might actually be the first medical office building. The Franklin House was located on the downtown square. Margaret Winroot leased it from 1828-1830. She apparently leased office space in the building to more than one doctor.

The *Adams Sentinel* noted that Dr. Smyser could "be consulted on Professional business at Mrs. Winrott's hotel [where] the most ample recommendations of his skill in SURGERY can be exhibited."

Another doctor, James Walker, would "set artificial teeth in the approved manner and will be happy to wait upon those who may honor him with their confidence."

The dawn of a new century saw a change in the way medical care was delivered in the county. The first Adams County Medical Society was organized in 1872, but "died of inaction" in 1894, according to the *Gettysburg Times*. However, Dr. C. L. Stevens of the state medical society began urging a reorganization of the society in May of 1904. Two dozen doctors answered the call in October and reformed the county medical society.

The society originally met in the Hotel Gettysburg and various other locations around the county to talk about medicine and the business of medicine.

"The method of removing a larynx, substituting an artificial voice box which enabled the patient to enunciate properly, was a subject of much interest in 1925 when these miracles of modern medicine and surgery were only doctors' dreams," the *Gettysburg Times* reported.

Once the Warner Hospital opened, the society moved its meetings there in 1921. The society also standardized medical rates throughout the county.

"Lively discussions of new standard office and obstetrical fees resulted in an increase in both. The amount of $20 was finally agreed upon in latter case and it entitled the patient to one additional visit, the office fee to be 75 cents," the *Gettysburg Times* reported.

House calls were originally 35 cents, night calls after 9 p.m. were 50 cents and overnight stays in the hospital were $10 a night.

Today, the county has hundreds of doctors serving the needs of residents.

The Annie M. Warner Hospital and Nurses' Home in Gettysburg, which eventually became Gettysburg Hospital. Courtesy of Wikimedia Commons.

ABOUT THE AUTHOR

James Rada, Jr. is the author of historical fiction and non-fiction history. They include the popular books *Saving Shallmar: Christmas Spirit in a Coal Town, Canawlers* and *Battlefield Angels: The Daughters of Charity Work as Civil War Nurses.*

He lives in Gettysburg, Pa., where he works as a freelance writer. Jim has received numerous awards from the Maryland-Delaware-DC Press Association, Associated Press, Maryland State Teachers Association and Community Newspapers Holdings, Inc. for his newspaper writing.

If you would like to be kept up to date on new books being published by James or ask him questions, he can be reached by e-mail at *jimrada@yahoo.com.*

To see James' other books or to order copies on-line, go to *www.jamesrada.com.* You can also sign-up to receive updates, news and free stories by joining his e-mail list on the site.

If you liked
BEYOND THE BATTLEFIELD,
you can find more stories at these FREE sites from
James Rada, Jr.

JAMES RADA, JR.'S WEB SITE
www.jamesrada.com

The official web site for James Rada, Jr.'s books and news including a complete catalog of all his books (including eBooks) with ordering links. You'll also find free history articles, news and special offers.

TIME WILL TELL
historyarchive.wordpress.com

Read history articles by James Rada, Jr. plus other history news, pictures and trivia.

WHISPERS IN THE WIND
jimrada.wordpress.com

Discover more about the writing life and keep up to date on news about James Rada, Jr.

12167427R00123

Made in the USA
San Bernardino, CA
10 June 2014